the ESSENCE of good horsemanship

the
ESSENCE
of good horsemanship

ross jacobs

This edition published in 2014 by Ross Jacobs

ISBN: 978-0-646-93090-9

Typesetting by *Wordzworth.com*

www.goodhorsemanship.com.au

Contents

FOCUS

CLARITY

SOFTNESS

RELATIONSHIP

THE LITTLE PRINCE

Acknowledgements

I wish to thank Marnie Ford and Ben Moxon for their editorial help and invaluably useful comments and corrections.

Most of all I owe a huge debt of gratitude to my wife, Michèle Jedlicka who has been my inspiration, cheer squad, advisor and (thankfully) my most brutal critic.

Lastly, this book is the result of lessons learned from my mentors, colleagues, students, clients and the many horses I have been privileged to experience. I have been incredibly fortunate and am very grateful.

Preface

One day I was driving on my way to a clinic. There was a discussion on the radio about a competition run by a charity in Melbourne, Australia. The third prize was a flat screen television. Second prize was a weekend in a luxury hotel. The first prize was two days serving in a soup kitchen at a homeless shelter. The organizer of the competition pointed out that both second and third prizes were just stuff. But first prize was happiness!

At a clinic a student was circling her horse on the lunge – around and around it travelled like an orbiting satellite. However, with each revolution the circle got smaller, the horse flexed tighter to the inside and the hindquarters scooted out. Eventually the horse stopped, squared up to her and stared as if to say, "Now what do you want?"

This was a pattern the pair had been repeating for months at home and something the owner wanted to stop. It was the reason she came to the clinic.

I talked to her about stepping her feet in the same direction she was asking her horse to circle. I explained that her energy should follow a concentric pattern to her horse's circle. Up until then, the owner had been walking to the right while the horse circled to the left and then walked to the left when her horse circled to the right. They weren't going together. The lead rope was the only thing that connected them. By walking to the left when her horse was circling to the right, she was both drawing the horse's thoughts to the middle and driving the hindquarters to the outside. This is why the horse continued to stop and face her with a puzzled look. It was doing everything she had asked of him, she just didn't know it.

I coached on her about how to get with her horse when lunging. Despite making a huge effort to get it right, I still had to regularly remind her that she was walking the wrong direction. Every time I mentioned it, she let out a gasp of frustration. She couldn't believe something so simple was so difficult. She didn't know how she was going to go home and explain to her husband that she had spent all this money going to a clinic to learn how to walk in a circle.

On the second day, she was doing much better, but I still had to occasionally remind her to get her feet going with her horse and not against him. Finally, in absolute frustration she let out a scream, turned to me and asked in an exasperated tone, "Why is this so hard? This is the hardest thing I've had to learn with a horse."

Because she was getting herself worked up about her dilemma, I decided to stop the work for a few moments and just let her relax in hope that her frustration and anxiety would subside.

I said, "Everybody finds this hard when they begin. At almost every clinic there is at least one person who finds walking a circle really difficult. But I don't think this is really the hardest skill anybody has to learn about horsemanship."

"Really? Well, what do you think is?" she asked.

"Well, I guess it all depends on the person. But for me, I think it was learning to let go of my ego. When I was a young bloke, it was very humbling to realize the world did not exist for me. I use to think horses were put on earth for my pleasure. When it came to horses, nothing was more important than bending them to my will. My skill as a horseman was measured in terms of how much I could get a horse to do. Both my value and self-esteem were wrapped up in how much success I had with horses in the eyes of others.

"It took me many years and some hard lessons to learn how stupid I really was. It won't take you nearly as long to learn to walk a circle."

There are a lot of skills that need to be sharpened and need to come together as a package in order for someone to become a good horseperson. Most of the skills are quite mechanical in nature and are developed by thousands of hours of practice and good guidance from mentors. But those skills are not the hard ones to learn. They just take commitment. They just take practice.

The hard skills to learn are the ones that require an inner change in us. I talk a lot about trying to change the inside of a horse whenever I am working with it. I believe by changing the inside of a horse, I can make their life better and more harmonious whenever people are in the picture.

I discovered that by focusing my aims more towards helping horses feel better on the inside, I also helped them perform better on the outside. However, more importantly, I also found a way to let go of my need to be in control all the time. My ego became less about what I could get a horse to do and more about what I could do for a horse.

I can get horses to do some really cool stuff. I have honed my skills to the point that I can impress a lot of people with what I can get a horse to do. But like the flat screen TV and the stay in a luxury hotel, that's just stuff. That is second and third prize.

For me, first prize is what I can help a horse to feel. Nothing feels better to me than helping a troubled horse feel less troubled. It is the coolest thing.

I have learned that happiness comes from relationships. And I have learned from the people I love and from animals that have passed through my life, that the best relationships are the ones where I want to give as much (or even more) than I take. It too is the coolest feeling.

The woman at the clinic finally did get her feet organized to walk in a circle. But I am still really curious how she explained what she did at the clinic to her husband.

Introduction

About This Book

I am not sure how to describe this book. It might help if I tell you what it isn't.

It is not a training book. It will not give you details on how to train a horse or fix a problem. You won't be able to use this book to find out how to get your horse into a trailer or stop him from biting you. Instead, it is a book of ideas about horses and getting along with them that come after many years experience, people I have watched and talked to, and horses I have worked with.

This is not a book you can read from cover to cover like a novel. You won't get to the last page and then know all you need to know about horses. There is a lot more to know than exists between these pages. Some of the ideas inside will only make sense when you are at a certain place in your horsemanship. You'll think you'll understand some of the concepts today, but next year they may have a very different meaning to you. Each time you come back to read a section you might discover something new or see it in a new light.

The book is not a presentation of rigorously tested scientific principles regarding horse behaviour and training. They are from my head and my heart. If they have no importance to you, that's okay. You may have a different set of ideas and principles that come from your head and heart.

Many of the concepts presented are not mainstream ideas. Some even clash with long established principles in the horse world. The book is not intended to create argument or controversy. It is simply to present ideas and my hope is that it will encourage people to think and ask questions.

The horse world is awash with training methods for every aspect of dealing with horses from handling foals to competing at the highest levels in any given sport. Ask ten people for advice on how to train or how to deal with a problem, and each eager helper with good intentions will give you a different answer.

Most training methods work to some extent. They may not work on every horse or in the hands of every person, but they exist because they achieved results for somebody at some time.

The overwhelming majority of approaches to training are aimed at achieving submission and obedience from a horse. We all want our horses to do what we ask, when we ask and how we ask. When we ride we don't want them freelancing and making decisions on their own without asking us first. It may make for a more interesting ride, but perhaps a more dangerous ride, too. Therefore, having control of the riding experience means being able to create a fair degree of submission and obedience from the horse. In the minds of most horse people, this is all they want from their chosen training method.

However, I see a problem with this from the perspective of the horse. When training submission and obedience into a horse becomes the priority, the nature of the horse is often left behind. Horses are thinking and feeling animals. They have opinions about what we do with them. Anybody who has spent even a short time around horses knows they have something to say. To make the goal of training a matter of obedience ignores those opinions and emotional needs of the horse. To a large extent, the horse now becomes a machine. Treating obedience as the training priority can kill the essence of what makes a horse a horse.

This is easy to do, because by their nature, horses are very submissive; it's easy to exploit that side of their personality for our own purposes. Could you imagine what would have happened to the first person that tried to ride a horse if horses had a personality more like a cat? We would not be riding horses today.

It's my view that good horsemanship shapes training in a way that benefits both the horse and the rider, rather than turn a horse into a submissive automaton. Good training should not squash any part of a horse's personality. It should keep the horse inside the horse.

I see this book not as a training book or even a behaviour book, but a book of ideas that need to be questioned and discussed by both the average rider and the professional community. It is my hope that it will get you thinking a little differently about your horse, and your approach to working with it, that will enhance your relationship, lead to better results and further your enjoyment.

Training From a Horse's Perspective

Good horsemanship is a way of working with a horse that benefits both the horse and the rider. In order to know what factors we need to build into the training that benefits the horse, we first have to understand how a horse views training.

Although, training is simple in concept, it is difficult in practice. This is because a horse's behaviour is motivated by a different agenda than a rider's.

A horse has no concept of the point of a particular exercise. It sees no long-term benefit to training. For instance, we ride circles to improve our horse's balance, straightness, strength and softness. We see long-term benefit for our horse in riding circles. However, from a horse's perspective there seems no point to riding circles. Compare that to tracking a cow, where the horse learns to focus on something to follow. Many horses will follow a cow with life and freedom (and perhaps even joy), because it has a natural curiosity and sees purpose in moving forward in order to explore that curiosity; something that is often missing when trotting circles in the arena.

To add a human perspective to this idea, think about dieting. If people put themselves on a diet, it is only because they view the long-term benefit as being good for them. But in the short term, dieting is not very pleasant and if people could not grasp the long-term benefits, nobody would ever voluntarily choose to cut back on eating. In the short term, the hunger one experiences would appear to be counter-productive to a person's safety and comfort.

Now back to the horse that only thinks in the here and now and has no long-term vision. A horse does not see the benefits in a square halt at 'X', being lead into a racing barrier, having its teeth rasped, being locked in a horse trailer, or even walking through a puddle that it could easily go around.

Since a horse does not automatically see such things as good ideas, it will be thinking of alternative ideas that it believes are more conducive to its safety and comfort. If a horse thinks loading onto a horse trailer or having its teeth rasped threatens its safety and comfort, its thoughts will be on ways to avoid these dangers. This is where people often get into a fight with a horse and use force to change the behaviour.

Therefore, the challenge of good horsemanship is to present training in a way that a horse sees as beneficial.

It is the nature of horses to give priority to safety and comfort as the key drivers of behaviour. A horse will give up its need to eat, drink, seek companionship and a myriad of other drives, if it perceives its safety and comfort are threatened. These are the strongest determinants of behaviour in horses.

This is because horses are largely emotional animals with behaviours governed by these emotions. There are very many scientific studies in the fields of ethology, neural anatomy and psychology to support this notion. Additionally, any person involved with horses, even for a short time, cannot avoid experiencing first-hand the way a horse's emotions can dominate its behaviour. In brief, a horse's emotions drive its behaviour.

Horses are unable to rationalize their feelings and tell themselves there is no need to be afraid or feel unsafe. The emotions are entirely experiential and horses are compelled by their instinctive nature to adjust their behaviour according to those emotions. Unlike humans, they don't have a choice.

Given the emotional nature of horses, we have the option to approach their training in either an adversarial way or a co-operative way.

This book is for those that seek a good relationship with their horse, rather than a slavish obedience. With that in mind, the bulk of this book is devoted to a discussion on the three pillars of good horsemanship, focus, clarity and softness.

It is my opinion that through focus, clarity and softness a horse's emotional need is catered for in the training process. Ensuring these elements are in place allows a horse to find emotional comfort, giving purpose and solace to working with us in a co-operative manner. Without them, both our relationship with a horse and its performance will unavoidably suffer.

Focus, Clarity And Softness

I will be discussing focus, clarity and softness, and the many variables that contribute to them in detail in the remaining sections of this book. However, for now it is important to emphasize that focus, clarity and softness form a triumvirate in the training of horses. They are interconnected in such a way that progress in one depends entirely on progress in the other two. They form the tripod that supports good horsemanship.

For the purposes of being able to write about focus, clarity and softness in a purely educational sense, I will attempt to discuss them separately. However, in good horsemanship they are not separable. For this reason, you may find some concepts are repeated in different sections where I feel it is relevant.

At this point it seems prudent to have a brief summary of focus, clarity and softness to describe what they are and why they are important.

Focus

According to the Webster dictionary, focus is "an act of concentrating interest or activity on something."

I think this is an accurate, bare bones definition of focus. However, I believe that when it comes to discussing focus in relation to horses, it is much more than just a convergence of interest. A horse's focus is always on what it is thinking. This concept has important ramifications in the training paradigm, because being able to direct a horse's thought is the starting point of good horsemanship.

A horse's focus is never complete. Like humans, horses have the ability to be attentive to more than one thing at a time. We are always competing with the shifting distractions for a horse. Furthermore, a horse's focus is often fleeting and changes constantly. It's not as if you have a horse's attention captured and held for the rest of the session. It can come and go so quickly we can sometimes feel like a kitten trying to catch light reflecting from a wind chime.

As I have already mentioned, it is the nature of horses to place a sense of safety above all other instincts. Evolution made them animals of prey, at the mercy of predators that stalked them. For this reason, they have a heightened sense of their surrounds, aware of everything around them and noticing anything that moves or is out of place. Horses regularly scan their habitat for things that don't seem quite right. They need to check out anything that is different.

This is why a horse's attention tends to be locked in for only short periods. Their innate survival instinct ensures their focus does not fixate on any one thing for too long unless it represents a danger or they feel unusually safe.

The expression, "When the student is ready, the teacher will appear", reminds us it is almost impossible to teach if the student is not attentive. When we are in the classroom ready to teach, we need the horse to be mentally in the classroom, ready to learn. That's the point of focus.

There is no purpose in starting a lesson when the student is not mentally present.

I don't believe it is realistic to expect a horse to pay 100 percent attention to us. Nevertheless, I do think it is possible to get close to 100 percent if we take the time in our training.

Often, we start with only a little focus from a horse, but the job of good training is to increase the amount of focus a horse gives us and increase the amount of time we have it.

However, a horse's focus alone is not very useful. We can't do much more than pet a horse whose attention is entirely fixated on us. Our ability to get a job done with a horse relies on our ability to direct a horse's focus to performing a job. The function of drawing a horse's attention to us, is so we can then direct it to something that we want a horse to do, like walk into a trailer, change canter leads or circle to the left.

Every task we present to a horse should begin with the horse thinking about doing it first. If a horse doesn't have the thought to do something before they do it, then convincing them will be a battle of wills. It is only when a horse has the idea to do what we ask will a horse feel relaxed and comfortable.

Therefore, in good horsemanship we talk about focus as a horse being attentive to us in order that we can then direct its thoughts and govern its movement.

Clarity

Clarity refers to the accuracy with which the brain of the horse interprets the intent of the human. The closer our intent is to the way the horse sees it, the clearer we are being. When our intent is unclear, a horse is left with guesswork about how to respond.

The function of clarity is to give clear and unambiguous answers in a horse's search for safety and comfort. When we are unclear, confusion reigns and the horse's response can be significantly different from what we intended. In addition, a lack of clarity creates a great deal of stress in a horse's life and makes the good relationship we desire an impossible dream.

To achieve a high level of clarity requires a strong focus from a horse. Yet at the same time, clarity sharpens a horse's focus. Very often, focus and clarity feed off each other.

Let me give you an example. If a horse is crowding you and pushing through the pressure from the lead rope, it is because its focus is elsewhere. Our presence and the feel on the lead rope are in the way of the horse's idea to be somewhere else. However, if we apply enough pressure to interrupt the horse's thought, not only does the horse's concentration shift to us, but the pushiness ceases too. It becomes clear to the horse that our presence is important. In the one action, we improve the horse's focus and we offer a clear message that our space should be regarded as important.

Softness

Softness is the culmination of focus and clarity. It is the third pillar that completes good horsemanship, and without it, a horse is no more than a subservient machine.

A horse cannot be made to be soft because it comes from the inside of a horse being comfortable with following a rider's idea through a strong level of focus and clarity. A horse cannot be coerced into softness, nor can softness be imposed.

Many people confuse softness with lightness. They believe if a horse is responsive to pressure, and obeys our direction with very little input from our aids, it must be soft. It is naïve to believe that anytime we don't have to pull hard with the reins or kick hard with our legs, our horse is soft. There is an important difference between softness and lightness. Confusing the two will only lead to a troubled relationship with a horse.
So to be absolutely clear:

- Lightness is a physical response to pressure
- Softness is an emotional response to pressure

These are two entirely different things.

A horse can be light, but not soft, because it can be highly responsive to pressure and at the same time feel troubled by it. It is normal for a horse that is like this to be so worried by pressure that it does anything it can to avoid or escape it. There is no requirement for a horse that is light to also be relaxed and calm.

Yet, a horse that is soft will always be light. It is responsive to subtle forms of pressure that do not trouble the horse. In fact, a truly soft horse gets comfort from pressure because pressure offers clarity to how it can find comfort. Therefore, a horse that is light to the aids is not necessarily soft, but a horse that is soft is always light to the aids.

In a light horse, pressure causes worry. However, in a soft horse pressure creates comfort.

I have already explained good horsemanship is about working with a horse's emotions. By coaxing a horse to be soft, we also help it feel emotionally comfortable. This goes a long way to building a good relationship and encourages a horse to offer its best.

In addition, softness inspires greater focus and improved clarity, because the calm emotions of a soft horse means a rider is not competing with inner turmoil and mental distractions. So once again, greater focus and clarity leads to greater softness, which in turn, affects focus and clarity in a positive way.

FOCUS

Everything A Horse Does Begins With A Thought

Summary: *Horses are not much different to humans in that the first part of taking an action is to have a thought to act. Everything a horse chooses to do begins with a thought.*

As I sit at my desk thinking what to write about the role of a horse's thought in training, it dawns on me that I am doing exactly what a horse does before it chooses to do anything. Before I type words on a screen, I think about what I want to say, how to use my fingers on the keyboard and how to lay out the page. All these thoughts play around in my mind before I am able to put words on the screen.

Horses go through the same process of thinking about what they will do before they do it. It's no different from you and I or any animal with a complex brain. Any activity a horse chooses begins with a thought. Before a horse wanders over to the trough for a drink, it starts with recognition that it is thirsty and a decision to go to the water. When a horse feels pain from a bad fitting saddle, it processes a thought on how to react before it bucks. If you ask a horse to pick up a foot, it thinks about shifting its weight to unload the foot before it lifts it off the ground. All actions begin with a thought.

The only exception to this is when a horse acts from reflex. When a horse has a reflex, there is no thinking or conscious processing of ideas. There is no recognition or decision making on the part of the horse. It just happens. However, in reality reflexes only make up a very small number of behaviours in horses. An example would be blinking when some dust is blown into an eye or coughing when the upper airways are irritated. However, in general an idea or mental processing precedes almost all horse behaviours.

Sometimes, the responses like shying or bucking can appear to happen so quickly that it seems like a reflex, but in reality that is not true. If a horse's response was a reflex they could not learn to modify their responses. If a horse shied as a reflex, no amount of experience or education would enable that horse to change its shying response. This is because reflexes cannot be trained. Yet, we know that horses can and do learn to modify their shying behaviour.

So such reactions, no matter how fast they appear to be, require some mental processing on the part of the horse.

A Horse Is Always Trying To Do What It Is Thinking

Summary: *The thought that most occupies a horse's thinking is the one it tries hardest to carry out.*

When we have a thought to do something, we usually try to do it. If it's an important thought like calming a screaming baby or answering the phone, we try to do it straight away. In a similar way, horses are always trying to act on their thoughts too. The idea that a horse views as the most important, is the one they most try to carry out.

Take for example when a horse is working in the arena. Most horses, particularly in their early training, will be drawn towards the arena entrance. Their walk quickens when heading towards the gate and slows when walking away from the gate.

When circling in the arena, a horse may fall out on its shoulder on the side of the circle closest to the gate and fall in on the circle on the side furthest from the gate.

Why? It's because the horse's primary thoughts are on the gate. The gate means back to the paddock and back to friends. Sometimes, the horse's thoughts are so strongly fixed to the gate that when the rider tries to force the horse away from the gate it may rear, or buck, or stop, or present with some other unwanted behaviour.

The importance that a horse places on an idea is what determines the urgency or desperation to carry out the idea. For example, many horses with insecurity problems can become very difficult or even dangerous if they are separated from other horses. The need to be with other horses can be so great that nothing else matters to a horse.

A horse's feet are controlled by its mind. Any idea that is at the forefront of a horse's mind is the thought a horse is trying to carry out with its body. The stronger the idea, the more desperately a horse will try to carry it out.

A Horse Must Change What It Is Thinking To Change What It Is Doing

Summary: *Since a horse is always trying to carry out what it is thinking, in order for it to act differently requires it having a different thought.*

If you accept that a horse is always trying to do what it is thinking, then it seems logical that if you want a horse to change what it is doing, you first want the horse to change what it is thinking. It is a fundamental tenant of good horsemanship that in order to direct a horse to do something we must first change its thought.

Without a change a thought, we are using force at some level and working with a horse that would rather be doing something else. It is not possible to have a soft and willing horse if we are directing them to do one thing, while they are thinking about doing something else. It results in second-rate performance and damages our relationship.

I have often said that the only change worth having is a change of thought. The rest is wallpaper for covering over resistance and emotional anguish. If a rider asks for something from a horse and there is no change of thought, there is trouble inside the horse.

People often confuse what a horse is doing with what he is thinking and feeling. They sometimes believe that if a horse is moving how it is directed, all is well. However, this is not always true because a horse can do what it is told while still holding onto its resistance.

When the horse's idea is the same idea we are trying to instill, the horse will perform with minimum anxiety and resistance. This happens because a change of thought creates a change in emotions, as the task is now the horse's idea. There is no need for the horse to put up a fight and argument against what we present because it now sees the new idea as the best option for safety and comfort.

Everything we ask of a horse should cause a change of thought, whether to stop, turn or go. It's equally true if we ask them to pick up a foot or load into a trailer or tie up. Nothing is more central to working well with a horse.

To Accept A New Thought, A Horse Must Let Go Of An Old Thought

Summary: *For a horse to be able to change its thought requires it to let go of the thought that presently occupies its mind.*

This is probably self-evident, nevertheless, we often don't realize that the problems we have with a horse are the result of a horse not being able to release the thought that occupies its mind at the present.

When you think about doing something, the only thing that causes you not do it is that something changes your mind. Maybe you realize it is too hard or perhaps something more important interrupts your idea. Whatever the reason, your first idea is blocked and no longer occupies the primary space in your thoughts. Another idea has replaced it. If you didn't let go of the original thought, you'd continue to try to make it happen.

It's exactly the same with horses. In order to have a change of thought, there has to be some letting go of the original thought. Once it lets go of an old thought it is open to accepting a new thought. That's the time we can be most effective in directing a horse's mind with a new thought and thereby get a change in the way it responds.

Most horses don't have trouble letting go of a thought if they are convinced the new idea is a better idea. Look at how easily a horse can be distracted from a job when a bucket of food arrives! The old thought is quickly substituted by the new thought because the horse believes filling its belly is a more important idea.

Now, turn the situation around and try to get a horse accept a new idea while it is eating its grain. The horse will be convinced that eating is far more important an idea than riding circles in the arena and will show a lot of resistance to changing its thought.

Most horses don't have trouble accepting a new idea from a rider once they can let go of their old idea. The stronger the thought, the harder it is for them to let go of it and therefore, the harder it is for them to accept a new idea. This is why most of us have trouble directing a horse. It's not that the horse won't take on board our attempts at directing their mind, it's just that it has a hard time giving up the idea that it already has.

Horses can have escalating thoughts, too. Imagine a horse that tries to go through a gate ahead of its handler. The horse is blocked from rushing through the gate because the owner doesn't want to get run over. By blocking the horse's feet from doing what the mind is thinking, the thought to rush through the gate can escalate and become stronger. The situation will not become safer, and may get even more dangerous, until the horse changes its idea to push through the gate and not trample the handler in the process.

The other side of the coin to this concept is that once a horse has an idea that it perceives is a good idea, it will jump through metaphoric hoops of fire to carry it out. It is a very important principle of training that when an idea has worked to the horse's benefit in the past, it will try and try to carry out that idea for a very long time, even though it appears the concept is no longer working to its benefit. It emphasizes how strongly a horse will hold onto an idea when it is sure it will eventually reap rewards.

This often gets in the way of training new behaviours. In order to overcome this, trainers need to develop strategies that are intended to substitute the horse's idea with one even more important to the horse.

Let's say my horse is prone to pulling back when it is tied to a post because it has a fear of confinement. I can choose to approach the problem by using techniques that instill a sense of futility and helplessness in my horse, such as tying it up with a strong rope and halter and letting it pull back as much as it wants until it gives up exhausted.

Alternatively, I can wrap a long lead rope around a post that will slide when my horse pulls back and allow the horse to move. In this way my horse learns it can move and is not confined. It no longer feels the need to pull back because it's changed its thought about needing to escape in order to live.

A horse is always looking for what it perceives is its best option. If it has already established a pattern of response, that's the response it will be trying to repeat for a very long time because it is convinced it is the best option. It doesn't matter if in reality, the response causes greater discomfort or not. Once a horse believes that its response will lead to more comfort and certainty of survival, it will repeat the pattern until convinced otherwise.

While on the subject of substituting one idea for another, I want to point out that when we re-direct a horse's idea to a new idea, the old idea is never gone. A horse does not put the old thought in the rubbish bin, and then give it to the garbage collector to destroy. The idea is still inside the horse, but it is no longer the primary thought.

We have trained the horse to have a new primary thought, but we didn't eradicate the old thought. This has implications for experiences that follow. It means that if the new idea stops working for the horse, it will go back and retrieve the old idea to see if it will work better.

As an example of this principle, imagine I am asked to ride a horse that is unresponsive to a rider's leg pressure because the owner has dulled the response by constantly kicking the horse every stride. With some work, I am able to re-train the horse to be responsive to leg pressure by making sure the horse understands the meaning of the feel of a rider's leg. However, when the owner rides the horse and once again begins to constantly kick the horse every stride, it will take no time at all for the horse to become unresponsive to leg pressure.

The training never eradicated the behaviour to ignore leg pressure; it just gave the horse a new way to respond to a rider's leg pressure. However, once the rider repeated the old pattern that caused the problem, the old pattern of behaviour will emerge. The original idea that we thought we had got rid of was lying just below the surface.

From the discussion so far, it would seem obvious that it is better to avoid a horse establishing patterns of responses that we don't want. Harry Whitney has a saying, "As they are started, so they will go". I believe he means that the first idea a horse learns about something is the one it will hold onto the strongest. It's the concept it will keep coming back to when the new ideas no longer profit a horse.

I think there are two conclusions we can draw from this. Life would be a lot easier if the first time we teach something to a horse we implant the right ideas at the beginning, rather than have to change them later. And secondly, it emphasizes the importance of being incredibly consistent in everything we do, in trying to ensure our thoughts and the horse's thoughts are the same.

How A Horse's Focus And Emotions Are Linked

Summary: *A horse's emotions drive its thoughts. The more relaxed and calm a horse feels, the more it is ready to have its thoughts and focus changed. It's hard to separate how a horse feels from what it is thinking.*

It is impossible to separate the way a horse feels from the way its thoughts operate. The feelings a horse carries play an integral role in determining the way its mind works.

Trainers are always talking about the value of having a horse with a relaxed mind, because a relaxed mind is more available for taking in new information. A horse that is relaxed is without doubt, in a more 'trainable' state than one that is running on adrenaline and high-octane nervous energy.

Too often, fear and worry cause the survival instinct of a horse to kick in, which sets up a barrier to the horse being able to focus and allow its thoughts to be directed. When a horse is worried, anything it perceives as a risk to surviving that experience is immediately looked on with suspicion and as a possible threat to its life.

When a horse feels its comfort and safety are not at risk, it can be like a sponge for learning. It sees, smells and hears everything, and all this information is compiled in its brain. However, while horses are so good at gathering information, they not so good at sorting it. The things we want them to know and the things we don't want them to know are lumped in together. Sifting the good from the bad is where our presence can be most influential.

We help horses find an emotional calmness from the things we want them to learn and a little emotional worry from the things we don't want them to learn. This concept highlights an interesting thing about anxiety.

When a horse feels a lot of anxiety, it hinders learning and gets in the way of the training process. Yet, when it experiences a small amount of anxiety, it aids in the training process by helping a horse to separate the behaviours that will be a benefit and behaviours that won't. For us, this might be the difference between the behaviours we want them to learn and the ones we don't want them to learn.

For example, sometimes I come across horses at clinics that are reluctant to move forward from a rider's leg. Very often it is easy to see the problem originates from anxiety and confusion about how to respond to leg pressure. When a small amount of leg pressure is applied, the small amount anxiety is enough to motivate a horse to try something close to moving forward. When this is rewarded, it opens to the door to more clarity and less anxiety, which can be built upon to gradually teach the horse to be comfortable in moving in response to a rider's leg.

However, sometimes people try to overcome a horse's resistance by being strong with their leg pressure. Very often this has the opposite effect of creating more anxiety and making the feet even stickier. The stress is too great for a horse to process and learn from what the rider is attempting to teach.

In general, I have found that the more sensitive horses are easier to train than the more dull ones. I think this is because their sensitivity means they are more motivated to search for safety and comfort than horses that are more stoic. They don't handle pressure and discomfort with the same ease, and are always looking for a better deal.

However, we are always balancing their state of anxiety between it being too much that it blocks their ability to think, or too little that they have no motivation to change their thoughts.

I remember riding my pony, Chops, who was a very sensitive and potentially reactive horse. She was constantly looking to me for what might be asked next. Her sensitivity made her great fun, and meant that once she got the picture, I rarely had to offer more than clearing of my throat to draw her thought back to me.

However, there was a time when we were riding on a trail on a beautiful summer's day. It was peaceful and quiet. Suddenly I heard a roaring sound coming through the trees towards us. It sounded like an engine. It was coming fast and getting loud. By the time I realized we were in a cloud of swarming bees, Chops was already taking off at high speed through the trees. There was nothing I could do to get her attention until we got a hundred metres or so from the bees. Her thought was gone and her body did everything it could to catch up to her thought.

So strong was her idea to save her life that there was no room in her mind for anything I was trying to get her do. It was not until Chops had put enough distance between her and those bees did the fear dissipate enough to allow room for her to hear what I had to say.

The point of this story is to illustrate that the strength of a horse's thought is determined by how convinced it is about whether it will live or die. It also illustrates the point that there is a threshold of fear that a horse hits and if it crosses the threshold there is nothing that can be done until the horse becomes calmer. On the wrong side of that boundary, a horse is incapable of listening or changing its thoughts until it believes safety has returned.

Being aware of the line between too much anxiety and just enough anxiety to motivate a horse to change its thought is an important element to being an effective horse person. If you cross the line to the wrong side, you might as well put your horse away for the time being and try again later.

Primary And Secondary Thoughts

Summary: *Focus is the first pillar of training and the first part of focus is having a horse's attention on us. We can't communicate with our horses if they are distracted. If we are not already a primary focus to our horse, we need to find a way to become more important than anything else.*

I have already briefly mentioned 'primary thought' in the previous section, but did not clearly explain the notion. This is a concept that my friend, Shea Stewart has talked about. It is the idea that a horse has multiple thoughts floating through its mind, but at any one time there is a primary thought. The primary thought is the one that ranks highest in importance. The primary thought can change and become a secondary thought and visa versa, but the point is, there is only one primary thought at a time that foremost occupies a horse's mind.

In the very early stages of training, the goal is to make the handler the primary focus. We want our horse to be primarily attentive to us and everything else to be less important. If we are going to influence and direct a horse's thought we need it to be focused on us more than anything else.

This does not mean that a horse should not be aware of its surrounds. It needs to be. We are always competing against the rest of the world for our horse's attention. However, there is a big difference between a horse noticing something and making that something the object of primary focus. Amid the chaos and babble of a horse's mind, I'd like my horse to be able to hear my quiet whispers.

Hard Focus And Soft Focus

Summary: *A soft focus is associated with a minimum of resistance, whereas a hard focus entails a high level of resistance. A soft focus can be manipulated and directed, but a hard focus is generally very fixed and not easily changed. In good horsemanship we are working towards encouraging a soft focus in a horse and discouraging a hard focus.*

These are terms I coined to describe two types of focus.

In a horse, hard focus comes from a place of worry. When a horse becomes concerned about something it will concentrate its attention out of concern for its safety. With a hard focus the horse displays a mental and physical tightness. The horse becomes fixated on something because it is too worried about what might happen if it takes its focus away.

A hard focus is often accompanied by signs of alertness such as raising its head, flaring the nostrils, short and shallow breathing, tension in the topline, a tight mouth etc.

I remember many years ago riding my Percheron gelding, China, in the gorge country of northern New South Wales. The sun was shining and the birds were singing and everything seemed right with the world. Suddenly China propped himself, raised his head and blew an explosive burst of air through his nostrils. His eyes fixed on something on the ground near a bush.

I couldn't make out what he was looking at. It just looked like a clump of dirt at the base of the bush. China refused to budge or be distracted from what drew his attention. After nearly a minute of this, I detected a small movement under the bush. It was an echidna trying not to be seen.

The disguise was almost perfect, but not perfect enough for China's keen powers of perception. There is no doubt that the echidna drew almost all of China's focus, but the focus came from a place of anxiety. It didn't come from good feelings or even curiosity. His focus on the spiny animal came from fear of taking his eyes away from the echidna. This was a hard focus.

In contrast, a soft focus displays almost none of the features of a hard focus. A soft focus does not come from worry, but from feelings of interest and relaxation. A horse will be attentive with a soft focus when it feels okay and its emotions are not driven by adrenaline. It is soft focus that we are trying to encourage in good horsemanship because it allows a horse to take in information and process new thoughts. Without a soft focus, directing a horse entails some degree of force, or bullying to make it perform.

The difference between primary and secondary thoughts versus hard and soft focus is that the concept of primary and secondary thoughts describes the importance and position those thoughts occupy in a horse's mind. Whereas, hard and soft thoughts describe the emotional attachment a horse places on those thoughts. A primary thought can be the result of hard focus or soft focus.

For example, with my horses, when LJ walks up to Guy to move him away from the food bucket, LJ has given Guy both his primary thought and hard focus. But when LJ approaches Guy for some mutual grooming, LJ has given Guy both his primary thought and soft focus. Either is possible.

Capturing A Horse's Focus

Summary: *In order to obtain focus from a horse, we need to make ourselves more important than all the other distractions in the world. By interrupting a horse when it is distracted, we help make the distraction less important and what we present becomes more important. In this way, a horse learns in time to keep its attention on the rider or handler.*

Now that we have talked about a horse's thoughts and its relation to focus, perhaps we should discuss the principles of capturing a horse's focus.

Capturing the focus of a horse is nothing more than having its primary thoughts on us. Like I said earlier, we are always competing with the outside world for a horse's attention. It is probably impossible to achieve 100 percent focus, but with each interaction with our horse we should strive towards it.

In order for our horse to be attentive to us it needs a reason. Something has to motivate it to let go of the thought it already has and turn its attention to us. We have to become more important than the object of its attention, but with a soft focus.

Sometimes we might have to present something as small as a movement of a finger or a shift of our weight, and other times we might have to do much more. How much we have to do will be determined by how strongly our horse is focused on something else. When people ask me how strong to get with a horse, my answer is "as strong as their thought is to ignore you".

So how strong is a thought? That's where experimenting and experience comes in.

A useful principle to consider when gaining a horse's attention is the idea of interrupting the thought a horse already has. If a horse is focused on something, by presenting a different idea to focus on, we interrupt the horse's attention. It causes the horse to momentarily pay attention to us, to see what we are presenting. Then if we interrupt the horse again by offering another idea, we once more draw the horse's attention for a moment.

In principle, by asking for something new every time a horse turns its attention away from us, we encourage the horse to draw its thoughts back to us. In this way, eventually a horse learns to maintain focus on us because it has learned that at any moment we might ask it to do something new. The horse understands that life is easier when it remains focused on the handler or rider.

Several years ago a woman rang me to ask if I would assess her horse. She had been given a 3-year-old Warmblood gelding that had just been started. She told me that every time she tried to walk him down the laneway the horse dragged her along and she didn't have enough strength to stop him.

When I visited her, I discovered the source of the problem was a breakdown in focus between the owner and the horse. The owner presented herself in a very unclear and confusing manner to her horse. The resulting anxiety left the horse convinced that the best way through the situation was to tune out and do its own thing.

When I felt the horse mentally drift away from me, I re-established communication with the horse by interrupting its thoughts. It began by leading the horse down the laneway and when the horse's focus left me, I would turn and go back in the opposite direction without hesitating or waiting to see if the horse was with me.

The sudden change in direction and my insistence that the horse came along interrupted the horse's idea to charge ahead.

With a few repetitions it learned that maintaining focus on me made its life less confusing and more comfortable. It only took about 10 minutes before the horse was leading politely, with very little effort on my part to remind it that life was easier when it paid more attention to me.

There is no doubt that in the beginning, changing direction on the horse rattled its world and created anxiety. However, I needed to worry the horse a little in order to motivate it to pay attention to me. I had to give it a reason why I was more important than charging down the laneway. By changing the program and interrupting what the horse thought it already knew, I was able to maintain the horse's focus on me.

To me, perhaps the most important message from this episode is how pressure, when applied with clarity, can be a comfort to a horse.

By the time I saw the horse, it had already been taught to ignore people and feel anxious by the owner's lack of clarity. Nevertheless, by using pressure in a different way to capture its attention and give meaning to my presence, I was able to bring comfort and clarity back into the horse's life.

With another horse, I might have done something completely different, or one tenth as much to get a change of focus, and yet another horse might require a whole lot more. We should always be striving to use the minimum amount of energy to get a change. Even so, we have to do enough.

However, there is a caveat to this principle. Sometimes we are the cause of a horse's lack of focus. We can present ourselves in such a way that a horse chooses to be mentally disconnected from us. The feelings that we induce in a horse can force it to want to be focused elsewhere. This is usually associated with a horse having hard thoughts, rather than soft thoughts.

When a horse struggles to redirect its attention towards us, we should consider the possibility that our energy or lack of clarity causes a horse concern and the belief that concentrating on us is a bad idea.

There is no benefit in doing less than enough, because without a change of thought, a horse will learn to ignore us. However, doing more than is required borders on punishing a horse. It increases a horse's anxiety to a level that is greater than necessary to motivate it to search for a new answer.

How Long Can A Horse Maintain Focus?

Summary: *There is some disagreement among horse people about how long a horse can maintain focus. In my view, the ability to remain focused is determined by how strongly motivated a horse is to be attentive to the human, who stands in competition with the many other distractions in a horse's life.*

I often get asked how long you can work a young horse. The presumption is that a young horse has a pretty short attention span, and therefore cannot be worked as long as an older horse. I know people who have a rule that 15 minutes is the maximum they would work with a horse under 12 months. I don't have any rules like that.

I believe that the ability of a horse to stay focused on any one thing comes down to how important it is to a horse. It's all about how we motivate a horse to pay attention.

For those that argue that nature gave horses only a short attention span, I suggest you try putting a bucket of grain in front of it to eat and see how many times it gets distracted before the bucket is empty. As long as eating remains the primary thought, a horse will not lose track of the bucket.

There have been several behavourial studies examining the attention span of horses, but each one that I have read failed to consider the importance of motivation, which is fundamental to the question of how long can a horse be attentive. I believe none of the studies are able to draw definitive conclusions and answer the question of how long a horse is capable of maintaining focus.

It's easy to turn a horse's brain off by drilling a particular exercise over and over, or by putting it into a no-win situation, where trying seems futile. Mixing up the work and always making sure each exercise finishes with a horse feeling more relaxed, has a lot to do with keeping a horse's focus, irrespective of the age.

There is no doubt that some horses are more easily distracted than others. However, it is equally true that the ability to keep a horse of any age interested in the work is often limited by our abilities and not their capacity to absorb information.

Training is largely a mental process, and if you keep that in mind, working horses will cause them no physical harm. It's all about presenting the work in a way that keeps them feeling interested and motivated.

How Can You Tell Where A Horse's Focus Is?

Summary: *Where a horse is looking is often a good indication of where its focus is directed. Furthermore, a horse will try to align its feet in the direction of its primary thought. The path of least resistance is when a horse is moving in the direction of its strongest thought, while the greatest resistance will be felt when a horse is moving in the opposite direction to its primary focus.*

I have experienced firsthand skepticism from people who question whether it is even possible to know what a horse is thinking. I can't say they are wrong because it is not something you can prove within scientifically acceptable certainty. That said, when you have your theories confirmed over and over again by the weight of circumstantial evidence, it starts to have meaning and I feel I can make certain conclusions with a degree of confidence.

A horse exhibits several ways of showing us where its attention is focused.

At clinics I try to teach people to observe where a horse is thinking. I try to get them to notice the horse's eyes. because very often, the thing that a horse is looking at is the thing that holds its strongest focus (primary thought). By recognizing where both eyes are looking, a person can gauge how much of a horse's attention is given to the idea the person presents.

The ears of a horse can also be significant indicators of where a horse is thinking. They will often swivel around to point in the direction of where their attention has been drawn. Sometimes, the ears will do this in unison. In fact, if both ears are pointing in the same direction this generally indicates a strong interest in something. Even so, often each ear will point in a different direction to indicate that a horse is scanning its environment, and its focus is divided.

As I said before, a horse is always trying to do what it is thinking. This is often manifested when a horse is trying to align its body in the direction of its primary thought. You can usually see a horse adjust its posture and the angle of its body to coincide with where its focus has drifted. A horse tries to turn its body to make it easier to see what has captured its attention, such as another horse calling from a nearby paddock.

When a horse's body is aligned in the direction of its strongest thought, it will display the least amount of resistance. Conversely, when a horse is pointed away from the direction of focus, you'll experience an increase in resistance. Therefore, awareness of when a horse's resistance changes will tell a rider a lot about where a horse's thoughts are directed.

One misconception a lot of people make is to mistake a tilt of the head or a bend of the neck as an indication of where a horse is primarily focused. In an ideal world this would be true.

Nonetheless, a horse can bend its neck or change the angle of the poll while continuing to focus in the opposite direction. For instance, when a rider picks up a rein to turn a horse to the left, many horses will flex their neck around to the left, but their eyes will gaze to the right because their primary focus is to the right. This will be reflected in the degree of resistance a horse presents to the left rein.

Criticism Can Hinder Focus

Summary: *There is a fine line between encouraging and discouraging a horse when we try to help them let go of one thought and replace it with another. We shouldn't tell a horse off for being too interested in the other things, but instead show it there is a more profitable idea worth thinking about. We shouldn't just criticize the horse for the sake of being critical. It's a far more positive approach to training and reduces the risk of teaching a horse to tune out or feel badly towards the work.*

We should be aware that it is perfectly okay that a horse's attention drifts from one thing to another. A horse will be aware of the bird in the tree, the feel of your leg against its ribs, the shadow on the ground, the smell of another horse on the wind, the sound of a barking dog in the distance and the stone it just stepped on all at the same time. While our objective is to encourage a horse to primarily focus on us, it would be a mistake to try to prevent it from being aware of all these other factors.

A horse is allowed to be a horse and we should not be trying to make it give up what it is to be a horse just to satisfy our desire to be more important. If you try to suppress the horse's need to be aware of the environment, you run the risk of causing it to shut down and mentally block out everything in its world – including you.

When you struggle to keep a horse's primary attention on you, view it as a chance to reinforce the importance of focusing on you rather than see this as a failure in the training. Every time we interrupt a horse from being distracted, we are reaffirming our importance in its life. It's only with repeating this lesson that it becomes established as a habit for a horse to always take an interest in us and what we present.

Nonetheless, there is a line between working to keep a horse's attention and driving it crazy by nagging. We need to find a way of presenting ourselves that inspires focus, but avoid making the horse feel it can do nothing right and that we are constantly critical. If a horse feels that it is always being criticized, it will have the opposite affect and encourage it to tune us out. Instead of training it to be focused and ready for everything we have to present, we will teach a horse to ignore us because we are always creating ill feelings through our criticism.

Each horse is different and the line between helping and criticizing will constantly change, so you have to find your own way through this maze.

A key element to ensuring that interrupting a horse's thoughts is a positive experience and not a negative one, is not to chastise for having a thought you don't want, but instead offer a new thought you do want. Some people try to gain their horse's focus by telling the horse it shouldn't be paying attention to something else. They say, "Don't look at that other horse" or "Don't be interested in that wallaby". They try to interrupt its thought by a flick of the lead rope or attempt to turn its head in the opposite direction. It's always don't, don't, don't.

A more helpful approach can be to interrupt the thought you don't want your horse to have with a thought you do want it to have. Rather than telling your horse that it shouldn't be interested in the other horses, you could present a different idea to it such as soften in your hand or line up along the fence or trot over a pole. Always be ready with a new idea to offer your horse.

The Human Focus

Summary: *When we try to gain and direct a horse's focus, we also need to be focused. In order to present our intent to a horse with clarity, we need to be disciplined in how we use our body language and cues. If a rider's mind wanders from the horse and the task, then clarity is diminished. It's not possible to obtain focus from a horse if we are not focused.*

Communicating with a horse is a two-way exchange between rider and horse. It's not uncommon for people to complain about their horse's lack of focus and find that the problem is their own lack of focus.

I remember one time going to a client's property to give a lesson to a teenage girl. Her arena was close to the road. She complained that her horse would shy away from the road every time a car or truck went past. I watched her ride for a while. The horse did shy at cars when it was ridden down the long side of the arena by the road. This happened a few times within several minutes.

I stood in one corner of the arena by the road, with a lead rope in my hand. The girl had to do a couple of laps of the arena before a car went past. As the car got nearly beside the arena, I gently twirled the lead rope in a circle as the horse headed towards me. Immediately both the horse and the girl looked at me. The car went past and I stopped twirling. The horse didn't even notice the car, and neither did the rider.

I had noticed that every time a car went by, the rider looked at it just before the horse shied. Her focus drifted from her horse and her riding, and she broke the mental connection between them. When I drew their attention to the twirling rope, the car was forgotten and there was no shying.

I had the girl keep trotting and told her to forget about the cars and trucks. Her job was to ride the horse on a line ahead of her. If she could maintain focus on the line she was meant to be riding, it would go a long way to helping her horse remain focused.

By paying attention to the cars and trucks she had taught her horse that they were important and something to watch. The distraction of the rider led to the shying.

In another instance, I once worked with a girl who was teaching her horse to work at liberty over some ground obstacles. The horse and the student were both on the same mental plane and working well together. The obstacles proved to be no problem once the mental connection was established.

Then her mobile phone rang. Still, everything was fine until she answered it. As soon as she started talking to the caller the horse looked away and wandered over towards the other horses. She broke the focus she shared with her horse, and gave it nothing to pay attention to. The horse wandered off to find something more interesting than listening to her owner chatting to a friend.

The concept of riders or handlers needing to be just as focused as the horse is so important. When I ride or handle my horse I am in that moment. I am aware of what I am asking and how it should feel when it comes out right. I don't start anything until I have a mental picture of what it should look like and feel like when it happens.

When I ask my horse to ride from point A to point B, I already know if I want a straight line or a zig-zag line; if I want to walk, trot or canter and how big a walk, trot and canter I want. I already know if I will stop along the way, when, and for how long. I already know if I will I want my horse with its head above, below or at wither height. I already know if I want to stop when I get to point B or turn around and go back or ride past.

I believe without this mental picture and level of focus in myself, I make it a whole lot harder for my horse to figure out what I am asking of it. Our own focus sets up our bodies through posture, muscle tension, weight shifts and energy to offer clarity of our intent to a horse through which we can direct their thoughts.

Directing A Horse's Thought

Summary: *Gaining a horse's attention is the first step to being able to direct its thought. However, there is no purpose to having a horse's focus unless we do something with it. It's important that once a horse is attentive to us, we then present it with another thought that gives purpose to why it should listen to us.*

When people first learn to ride they are generally taught that kicking a horse makes it go and pulling on the reins makes it stop or turn. Some people never graduate beyond that level of under-standing no matter how many years they ride. However, it is important to understand that riding and training is primarily about influencing what a horse is thinking, and allowing the horse's feet to follow its thought. For this to happen, a horse needs to hear it when we speak to them.

Up until now I have mainly discussed the idea of capturing and holding a horse's focus on us. I want to stress the very important point that the only purpose of having a horse's focus is to be able to direct it towards a task.

Having a horse's focus on us is like having money. The only purpose of having money in your pocket is so you can spend it; otherwise it is just occupying space. Yet you can't spend it until you first have it. It's the same with a horse's attention. There is no point in having a horse's attention unless you are going to direct it. However, first you need to have a horse's focus before you can direct it.

If a horse is distracted and is thinking about other things, it won't be aware when we want it to do something. When we tell it to trot for example, it needs to be listening. Without listening there can be no directing. Therefore, the first part of working with a horse's focus is to gain it and the second part is to direct it in relation to a job.

Let's look at the problem of lunging a horse. Often times, when a person is attempting to lunge a horse in a circle, the horse either turns to face the handler in the middle or pulls away to escape the handler. In either case, the horse may be attentive to the human, but its focus is not on moving forward on the arc of the circle.

Lunging correctly means a horse is focused partly on the person in the middle of the circle and partly on the line of the circumference of the circle. Only in that way can a horse be listening to us and at the same time travel in a proper circle.

In the training of a horse's focus we are not only working on getting the horse to be mentally connected to us, but also working to direct some part of a horse's focus to a task.

The Difference Between Directing And Driving A Horse

Summary: *In good horsemanship, our aim is to direct a horse's thoughts to encourage it to move in the way we intend. But it is very common that people will drive a horse rather than direct a horse. Driving tends to create undesirable feelings inside a horse because it often involves separating what a horse is doing from what it is thinking.*

I believe the difference between directing a horse and driving a horse is the difference between asking and making it do something. It's the difference between a horse feeling okay inside and a horse feeling troubled. I'm going to discuss more about directing versus driving in a moment, but first I will offer a definition of what I mean.

Directing
When you direct a horse you are moving it towards a thought.

Driving
When you drive a horse you are moving it away from a thought.

Driving is usually associated with a horse's thought being focused in one direction while its feet are moving in another. For example, if we drive a horse in a round yard, we apply pressure behind the horse by swinging a rope or using a whip, in order to get it to escape forward away from the pressure. The horse will believe the pressure is a bad thing and therefore moves away to avoid it. The horse's focus is on the pressure behind. Instead of thinking of going towards something, the horse is thinking of fleeing away from something.

On the other hand, if we were to direct a horse to move around the yard, we would encourage it to think ahead, not behind. We wouldn't be chasing the horse to move, but instead directing its thought forward in an effort to get the feet to move and catch up with that thought. In this scenario, the horse would be moving towards its thought and not fleeing from the pressure coming from behind.

Another example might be when asking for hindquarter disengagement. If we swing the tail end of the lead rope to apply pressure to the left flank of the horse to get it to disengage the hindquarters, we would be driving the horse away from pressure. The horse's thought would focus on the swinging lead rope and it would disengage the hindquarters to the right in order to escape from the pressure.

Alternatively, if I used a feel from my lead rope to ask the horse to look to the left and directed its thought to the left, it would disengage the hindquarters to the right in order to align its body towards where it is thinking. The hindquarters would disengage to follow a thought. There would be no tension or ill feeling because it was the horse's idea to disengage the hindquarters.

There is immense difference in the feel that a horse experiences when we drive versus when we direct its thought.

In the case of driving a horse, we are separating a horse's feet from its thought. When a horse's feet and its thoughts are in two different places, there is trouble inside. However, directing a horse entails encouraging a horse to move towards its thought and not away from it. The difference is critical in determining the final outcome and the quality of relationship we develop with our horse.

In every discipline, people talk about the quality of a horse's movement. In dressage, reining or western pleasure, competitors are scored according to the quality of the movements. As a result, people have come to assume that the focus of training needs to be on the obedience of the feet. When they do this, they forget that the horse's feet are controlled by a horse's mind.

Our reins, legs and seat do not control the feet. They only act as messenger of a rider's intent, which the horse's mind interprets and then directs the feet to move in a specific fashion.

The quality of the movement is determined by the emotions of a horse. A horse that is worried will have thoughts of tension and resistance. This leads to movement that exhibits tension and resistance. The opposite is true of a horse with a quiet and calm mind. Most of the time, driving leads to moving a horse while at the same time creating tension.

I believe that in good horsemanship we should strive towards the day when all our work entails directing a horse's thought and not driving its feet. Nevertheless, even when we use the movement of the feet to address a change in a horse's emotions, we should still prioritize a change towards calmer emotions as the most important aspect of educating a horse.

How Do You Know When A Horse Changes Its Thought?

Summary: *When a horse is thinking about one thing but doing something else, there is always some degree of resistance. However, when a horse changes its idea to something closer to our idea, there is always a decrease of the resistance. Alterations in a horse's resistance/ softness tell us a lot about changes in its thinking.*

To know if any changes coincide with a change in a horse's understanding, it is a good idea to repeat the exercise to test whether the change in thinking is reproducible.

In order to know when to release the pressure and reward a horse for a change of thought, you have to first know what a change of thought should feel or look like. This is not always easy and takes some experience.

When a horse changes its thought, it is always followed by a change in the resistance and the feel it offers to the rider or handler. If we stay aware of the feel a horse offers us, we can monitor when its thoughts and focus change.

Let's consider a simple example.

Say you want to teach your horse to move forward from a lighter feel of your leg. You might begin by asking very lightly with your leg, and if you don't get close to the response you hoped, you might use firmer leg pressure to elicit the forward response you had in mind.

Now the question is, when your horse went forward how can you be sure the horse made a real change in its thinking? How can you be confident the horse understood the lesson?

In my view, the easiest way to test if your horse had a change of thought is to repeat the exercise again. If you again apply a light leg pressure and your horse went forward as you hoped, then you can be sure there was a change of thought and your horse learned from the exercise. However, if you had to apply just as much pressure the second time as you did the first time, your horse did not learn the meaning of a light leg pressure from the exercise. There was no change of thought.

When you work through a resistance with a horse and get them to let go of their thought, it is a very important to always repeat it until you get a better response. It is the only way you can be sure the lesson was actually understood or whether it needs to be repeated again.

As a general rule, I believe we should never leave a horse feeling the need to resist the rider and we should always check that any change we achieve is repeatable. If we keep to those rules, the new way of thinking will become gradually ingrained in a horse until one day it becomes a way of life.

The Problem Of Routine

Summary: *Horses can be comforted by routine. But at the same time, a routine encourages a horse's focus to drift. This has consequences for engaging with a horse's mind.*

Horses find a great deal of comfort from knowing what to expect and the answers to problems we might present. They don't like surprises. For this reason they often look for patterns in the work we do with them. Patterns can help a horse gain confidence.

However, there is a danger to patterns. When we repeat exercises over and over again we can fall into the trap of creating a routine. When this happens a horse can perform the pattern with less and less mental effort until eventually it is working on autopilot. The obedience is there, but the mental engagement is absent.

The negative consequences of riding a horse that is just going through the motions can be mild or extreme. The worse cases I have seen involved horses that regularly bolted or severely shied when anything interrupted their ability to tune out.

Over the years, I have dealt with countless horses that failed to mentally engage and simply went through the motions. It's caused me to come up with several different strategies, but the principle is always the same. When a horse is mentally shutting out the human, but going through the motions, it needs a reason to open its eyes wide and take an interest in proceedings. Sometimes a horse's world needs a little shaking up, but without causing the survival instinct to spike. The comfort it gets by repeating a well-understood routine needs to stop being so comfortable.

Let me give a human example that might help. I owned a Nissan 4WD for about 16 years. It had done nearly 500,000kms. When I got in the car I didn't have to think how to start it or how responsive the pedals were or where the light and turn switches were located. I just got in and drove without giving any thought to what I needed to do because the pattern was so well implanted into my brain.

But then I bought a second-hand Citroën.

It was a wonderful car to drive. As expected, the feel was very different, but also, the Citroën switches were on the opposite side of the steering wheel to the Nissan. So for the first couple of trips, I was turning on the windscreen wipers when I wanted to indicate I was turning a corner. When I went to stop, the car would screech to a halt because the brakes were more responsive than I was used to in the Nissan. I realized that when I got in the Citroën I had to pay a lot more attention. Even when I drove the Nissan again, I had to pay attention and remind myself that it was not the Citroën. I was more aware of what I was driving. My complacency had been rattled a little.

If we think about a horse that is a little complacent in its routine, it's obvious we need to shake it up, too. One easy way is to not have a routine in our work. Routine kills a horse's interest. So make sure you are not forming habits that encourage a horse to work on autopilot.

But I want to suggest you think about other approaches to your training that introduce novel ideas to your horse.

For instance, a woman brought a horse to a clinic that would go on and come off her horse trailer, but there was a rush about it. Her horse was very obedient, but worried. The worry caused the horse to hurry its steps. The horse knew the routine of loading onto the trailer, but without engaging its mind in the process.

I decided to break up the routine of loading and unloading. Rather than ask the horse to load into the back of the trailer, I asked the horse to put one foot on the ramp and stop. This worried the horse tremendously at first because I had broken up what it thought it knew, which was to rush into the trailer. I got in the way of the thought to load into the trailer in the normal fashion.

When it stood quietly, I asked the horse to back the foot one step and stop. Then I asked for the other foot on the ramp and stop. When the horse offered a quiet moment, I asked that the foot be taken back a step. Then I asked for the first foot to make two steps onto the ramp and stop.

Bit by bit I built it up so the horse would step forward one foot at a time or back off one foot at time. Just when it thought it knew what I was about to ask, I changed it and asked for a different step or different direction.

I shook up the horse's world. The result was that not only did I help the horse's obedience, but I also helped its focus and the tension dissipated as it became more mentally engaged.

The concept behind that approach can be applied to almost any aspect of training. The list of ways I have tried to help horses engage in the training process over the years is a very long list. But the exercises themselves are not important.

The principle is to present something to a horse that it does not automatically know the answer to and let it find the answer. Don't impose the answer on a horse because then it won't need to think. Rather than having obedience, focus and softness, you'll only have obedience.

It's another one of those fundamentals of training that when we talk, we should convince a horse that it should listen. When I ask my horse something, it should matter to it and not cause it any bother. It should stimulate a horse to interact with me and search for an alternative way to respond.

CLARITY

Surviving Training

Summary: *Part of being able to offer clarity to a horse is to understand the horse's view of pressure in terms of survival. It is the job of training to convince a horse that the ideas we present do not threaten its survival.*

Clarity changes the way a horse views training. It brings willingness to a horse in working with us that would be absent without clarity.

Before I enter into a detailed discussion of the factors that contribute to clarity, I think it wise to first consider training from a horse's point of view. I believe an appreciation of how a horse sees what we do, can give an insight into both why horses behave as they do, and why clarity is such a vital component of good horsemanship.

Life and death! That's what horsemanship is to a horse.

We lovers of horses are pretty lucky. We get to choose our horses, we choose the amount of time we spend with them and how that time is spent. We pay money to a stranger, go into a paddock to catch a horse, which we then load into a trailer. We drive to an unfamiliar location, unload the horse and release it into a strange new environment. We watch it explore its new home while our heart is filled with the joy of our new acquisition.

Meanwhile the object of our happiness is lost and bewildered, its life has just been turned upside down and it is left wondering if it is going to die in the next few minutes. Everything the horse has known and felt safe about has changed. It is Alice in a terrifying Wonderland.

I think it is so easy for us to remain oblivious to what we put our horses through, simply because they are not running wildly and showing the obvious signs of panic. The things that seem small and insignificant to us are often terribly important to our horses. This is because everything a horse does is in some way tied to its sense of survival.

Our lives are made up of decisions that for the most part are choices about what we want. Do we go on holidays in August so we can go skiing or do we holiday in January to visit relatives? Do I want to sit on the couch or in the chair? Do I wear the blue sweater or the brown one? Do I send the kids to this school or that school? Do I order the fish or the beef?

This life of choosing what we want based largely on preferences is not something that horses get to experience very often when interacting with humans. Their decisions on what to do are based almost exclusively on their perception of what offers the best chance of living through the experience. Survival is the most important motivating factor in any behaviour offered by a horse.

When a foal is haltered and asked to lead forward for the first time in its life, its initial response will be to pull away and flee for its life. At the very least it will lean back against the pressure and at worst it will run back hard, and may even flip over backwards.

This behaviour is nothing more than the foal realizing that if it is going to live through this experience, it had better fight and get away from the pressure, otherwise harm is only moments away. To us it may seem a silly response for the foal to fight the lead rope because we know that if it only took a step forward it would feel better. However, it would be a mistake to underestimate what a terrible, life-threatening situation it has been put in.

In my mind, it is no less threatening than if a person pointed a loaded gun at me and demanded something that I couldn't understand. I wouldn't know what they wanted, but I knew I might die any second so I had better figure out something to get out of the predicament.

Horses face this dilemma every day when we handle them. Not too many older horses that have had a lot of handling react exactly like the foal when asked to lead. Even so, those types of situations occur for each horse all the time.

There are an infinite number of scenarios that evoke a strong sense of survival in a horse each day. Some are obvious, like shying at a motorbike coming around the corner or bucking when it has a sore back. Other situations are less obvious, but nonetheless real.

For example: trouble controlling the horse's speed; a horse's resistance to the reins; trailer loading taking two minutes instead of two seconds; fidgeting when tied up; being distracted or crowding the handler when it is being led. The list goes on and on.

All these behaviours are in some way strongly tied into a horse's sense of survival.

Why is it important to stay aware of this? Because awareness about what motivates a horse's behaviour goes a long way towards adopting an approach to training that does not evoke a strong 'life or death' type reaction from a horse.

We will always be asking our horses to do things that they initially feel are not in their best interest. Even so, there is a difference between asking for something that they feel threatens their life, and asking them to do things that are a bit hard.

I believe the best we can hope for is that our horses learn to be emotionally comfortable with what we want them to do. They may never learn to love the work, but they can learn to feel unstressed about it and find peace in working with us. For this to happen, we must develop a level of trust in our relationship with our horses. This takes a lot of time and a correct attitude to the training. It means avoiding, as best you can, putting your horse in situations where it feels it might die, and making every effort to ensure it feels better after you asked something of your horse than before you asked.

Telling a horse to do something that it feels will get it killed tells the horse that you can't be trusted with its survival. In time, a horse learns to associate people with threats to life and limb. Even if it gets through it, the level of fear and anxiety the horse will experience will damage the trust and confidence in you for a long time.

I think the traditional form of sacking out a horse is a good example of this. This is where a horse is tied to a big post with a big halter and a big lead rope and exposed to scary objects (like water from a hose or chaff bags with tins inside) until it stops fighting to get away. This type of training is called 'flooding' and it does not take into account how a horse feels inside.

All training has some level of flooding (such as buckling the girth on a horse for the first time), but it can be done in a way that helps the horse feel less stressed by first preparing it for the flooding.

Training cannot squash survival instincts. If a horse thinks it is going to die, all the best training in the world is not going to change what it does next. Fear and anxiety are what makes working with horses so difficult at times. If you approach training by trying to minimize the fear and helping a horse to feel relaxed, you are on the path to having a good relationship with your horse and getting the best that it has to give.

The Importance Of Teaching A Horse To Search

Summary: *Searching is the ability of a horse to explore various options of behaviour. Rather than using pressure to impose a specific behaviour on a horse, training should encourage a horse to search a range of responses. In this way, a horse will have discovered how to find the pathway to an answer itself, without being forced. The result is a clearer understanding and a frame of mind that inspires a horse to keep trying.*

Understanding the importance of a horse searching is perhaps one of the most important concepts in good horsemanship.

We can ask a horse to do something in a way that encourages it to search for a way to respond, or we can ask it in a way that discourages any searching and replaces it with blind obedience.

The latter leads to a domineering relationship with a horse and slavish performance, while the former can build the confidence in our horse to search for a pathway to the response we want it to understand.

The way in which most horses are pressured into a specific behaviour is by removing their choices. It entails narrowing the choice a horse has to find relief from pressure to one option. Anything other than the option the trainer wants is unacceptable, and often the pressure persists or may even increase. Almost always, relief only comes because the horse stops resisting, and not because the trainer removed the pressure.

Think about the horse that won't stand still to be mounted. It's common that these horses are made to stand still by fitting hobbles to their legs or having their nose pointed deep into a corner of the arena or flexing their neck around or holding both reins tightly. Standing still is forced upon the horse because the only relief comes from the horse no longer fighting.

However, when a horse is asked to do something and allowed to try different options, and it chooses the one we want, it is still the horse's choice. The meaning to a horse is very different to the one where it had no choice. It's the difference between learning a more comfortable way to respond for itself versus having a response imposed on it.

I believe training a horse to search has an important consequence that leads to greater clarity. It allows the horse to try options we didn't want it to try, discover for itself they weren't particularly good ideas, and scratch them off the list for the future.

The corollary of this is when it hits upon the thought we did want it to try, it owns that thought. The new thought makes sense to the horse, and because of that, it stays with a horse longer and is more reproducible. A horse that finds comfort through exploring various options will have a much clearer understanding of the job than one where it is forced to behave in a particular way.

Having said all that, we have to accept that it is okay if a horse chooses behaviours we don't want. A horse can't be blamed for exploring the possibilities and making decisions we don't like. The onus is on us to make our idea the easiest option for a horse to choose.

Making The Right Thing Easy

Summary: *A basic principle of good horsemanship is that how a horse responds to our aids is its decision. What a horse is thinking of doing and what it actually does do should be the same. A horse chooses a specific behaviour because it views it as the easiest response available to it. Therefore, to inspire a horse to have a new thought involves making the old thought a little less easy, and the new thought as close as possible to the old thought, while still being nearer to what we want. Good horsemanship requires asking a horse to make incremental changes at a time rather than paradigm shifts.*

"Make the wrong thing difficult and the right thing easy." Most of us have heard this many times. Most of us believe we know what it means and why it is relevant to training horses. However, I don't think a lot of people give much thought to what 'easy' means.

It's widely believed that 'easy' should be as easy as possible and 'difficult' should be slightly more difficult than easy. In order to know what is more difficult than easy, it seems that knowing what 'easy' is would be a logical pre-requisite to knowing how difficult 'difficult' needs to be.

To examine the question of what is easy we need to see it purely from a horse's perspective.

When we ask a horse to do something, the response it gives is the one it views as the best option among all the choices available to it. So in a horse's mind, what it is already doing is the easy thing. To ask a horse to change its response is to ask it to do something that it sees as being more difficult than the response it is already doing.

If we accept that a horse chooses its response from a belief it is the easiest (and safest) choice, then in order to alter the response by making the new response easy, we should try to make the newly desired response as similar as possible to the one the horse is already doing. This makes the choice we want the horse to make easier to find and feel more comfortable about.

For instance, imagine you are riding a horse that does not understand to move off a rider's legs. You apply your legs to the sides and the horse refuses to move except to swish its tail and toss its head. The refusal to move is a horse's response to confusion about how to respond to a rider's leg pressure. The horse sees not moving as its best option. Yet, we want the horse to walk, trot and canter when we apply leg pressure. So how do we get a change that is close to what the horse is doing, yet still getting closer to what we want it to do?

In a horse's mind, the second easiest option will be the next thing it tries when it decides not moving is no longer the best option. So we could try weighting that choice in our favour by perhaps using one rein to tip the horse's thoughts to the left after we apply a small amount of leg pressure.

If the thought goes to the left strong enough, the horse may shift its front feet to the left, and we would rejoice at the change.

If we repeat this exercise a few times, the horse will gain confidence that stepping the front feet to the left is now the easiest option when we apply leg pressure. Then it becomes time to ask for a bigger change by asking for more steps to the left and not making only one step the easiest option.

When more steps become the easiest option, then we might ask for the hindquarters to move too, and that becomes the new easiest option. In time, we build up these incremental changes in a horse's mind as to what is the easiest choice, until the horse is walking, trotting and cantering in response to our leg pressure.

I know many people use the idea of breaking down training into small steps to achieve a final result. However, I don't think everybody understands that what defines a step as being tiny enough is determined by how close it is to the thought a horse is already following.

The greater the gap between the thought a horse has and the thought we want it to have, the harder we make for it to choose our idea.

A Try In A Horse

Summary: *Building a try in a horse is a huge part of any training. The level of try determines the trainability of a horse. The approach we take in our training can either improve the try, or it can kill it. It is important that the try in a horse is always improving in order to avoid stagnation and mediocrity.*

This is probably a good place to briefly talk about what a try is in a horse.

When a horse is trying, it is searching for a way of removing the discomfort that pressure can bring. Searching is the act a horse uses to find the behaviour that will give relief from pressure. The stronger a horse is motivated to search, the stronger is the try.

Horses that are highly trainable have a strong try to search for an answer, but horses with a weak try are often harder to train because the care-factor about pressure is poor.

An example of this happened a few years ago when a woman sent a horse to be started under saddle. She had recently purchased the horse from the breeder. When asked why she bought the horse, she said it was because it was so quiet.

The woman told the story about her visit to inspect the horse and saw it standing in the paddock. The breeder walked up the horse and put a halter on it, then climbed on its back. The horse stood quietly, ignoring the owner. She told the woman that she had not done much with the horse at all, and nobody had sat on its back before. The woman was so impressed with the temperament of the horse that she decided to buy it.

This story immediately rang alarm bells for me. This is because the woman missed the tell-tale signs of a horse that would appear to have very little try. If a horse, with very little handling, didn't care about the first time a person sat on its back, why would it care when somebody applies leg pressure and asked it to move or picked up the reins and asked it to stop or turn?

If the care-factor is so low when somebody gets on it the first time, what will the care-factor be like when a person starts asking it to do jobs it doesn't think is a good idea? How much pressure would a person need to apply to inspire a horse like this to search for a different response? I was right to be concerned and the horse did prove to be quite difficult to start.

The second aspect about the nature of a try is that it should be constantly changing. Building a try in a horse is like building focus, softness, stamina, confidence, strength etc. The try in a horse should improve with further education. Sometimes people forget this and the level of try a horse offers today is the same level of try it offered weeks, months and years earlier. What was a good try in the past should no longer be considered a good enough try today if the horse is to improve.

A lady brought a horse to a clinic a little while back. This was probably her third experience at one of my clinics. I noticed that she had done a good job working with her horse on some basics we had covered at previous clinics. The horse was doing everything she asked, but I noticed her horse was a little tuned out and appeared to be working on autopilot. I mentioned this to her and added that while her horse was politely obedient, she also needed his mental participation if she wanted any sort of quality to the work.

What I noticed she had been doing was rewarding her horse for the same thing we had done at the last clinic six months earlier. She told me that she thought she was supposed to be rewarding the smallest try.

I explained that rewarding the smallest try is always desirable, but what was a try six months ago is now something her horse does while half asleep. It's no longer a try. If anything, the mental effort the horse contributed to working with the rider was significantly diminished from the effort of six months earlier.

A try should always be a moving target. Once a horse understands the job, then our expectations of how it performs the job should change. If we want a horse to improve, we need to move the goal posts of our expectations. This means providing clarity about where the new goal posts exist. There is no moving forward without pushing the boundaries as the horse progresses and becomes ready.

The Elements Of Clarity: Timing, Feel, Balance And Consistency

People often talk about timing, feel and balance as the keys to being clear in our training. I'd like to add consistency as the fourth element, because I believe we need to be consistent in our timing, feel and balance if we are to offer horses clarity.

This section discusses each of them, but any examination of these four elements is pointless without appreciating that they are closely interconnected. Each affects the others. Any adjustment of one automatically impacts on the others.

Timing

Summary: *For me, the best description of good timing is the time gap between a horse having the thought we want it to have and a new and different thought. The concept of timing not only involves when to release pressure, but also when to apply pressure. The better the timing we have, the easier it is for a horse to make the link between our request and the desired response.*

The simplest definition that I know is that timing is the judgment by a rider of when something should be done. I believe good timing means capturing the moment between when a horse has the thought we want and a new thought we don't want.

When most people think of timing, they think of the time delay between a horse doing something and our response to what it did. If a horse did it correctly, we respond with a reward or relief from pressure. If it did it incorrectly, we might ask again or impose a correction.

Horses tend not to hold onto a thought for very long because there is always another thought waiting to occupy its space. If we want to teach a horse a behaviour, the reward for the correct behaviour needs to follow soon after in order for the horse to associate that it received the reward because of the response it gave.

The smaller the gap between the horse's correct response and offering a reward (see the later discussion on Pressure for a description of what constitutes a reward), the easier it is for a horse to figure out that its response triggered the reward and a horse will learn that pathway more quickly. In principle, the longer the delay, the more difficult it is for a horse to connect the behaviour with the reward.

Some trainers even put a number on how long a delay a horse's brain can associate a reward with a particular response.

I've heard anything from three seconds to ten seconds is the maximum limit. I don't know how these numbers were derived.

Personally, my experience suggests there is no number. I believe the shorter the lag between a response and its associated reward the better, but I believe too many factors play a role in determining a workable lag time between response and reward for there to be a definitive cut-off point.

If we want to reward a horse for a change of thought, then the reward must be given before a horse has a moved on to another thought. If we delay the reward, the horse will have a different idea than the one we wanted by the time it received the reward. In that case, we will have rewarded the horse for the wrong change of thought.

It may take many moments before a horse considers other options, and to interrupt that flow of thoughts during the searching period might inadvertently discourage the response we want.

A common example of this is when a horse is asked for something and seems stuck at doing nothing. Many horses get a sleepy expression on their face and stand idle or frozen. However, it is often a mistake to assume those horses are not searching, because sometimes they offer the precise response you were wanting after quite a long time of appearing to be asleep.

With this in mind, timing can be affected by the horse's motivation to search for a relief from pressure. The more desperate a horse is to find a way out of pressure, the quicker its thoughts will come and go. The timing of the release from pressure is more crucial in sensitive horses that search harder for a way out. The urgency to search for a release from pressure is a reflection of a horse's sensitivity to the level of anxiety that pressure creates and the level of comfort a release of pressure offers.

There is an old joke about why so many people have trouble getting along with Arab horses compared to Warmblood horses. The joke goes that when you ask an Arab to do something it may have ten options to search through, but it will do them in five seconds. By the time most people realize the Arab tried the option they wanted, it has already moved onto other choices. So they reward for the wrong try, are always too late, and drive the Arab into frustrated insanity.

On the other hand, a Warmblood will have the same ten options, but it will take ten minutes to try them and most people can keep up with that. Of course it's just a joke and does not reflect reality, but it does point out the important principle that good timing can be different for different horses.

Another part of training that comes under the umbrella of timing is to know when to ask something of a horse. I have just talked about timing as the relief from pressure, but the timing of asking or applying pressure is also important.

To give an example, let's examine using the reins to step the left front foot of a horse to the left as it walks forward. A horse decides where it will land a foot on the ground before that foot leaves the ground. If a foot is in mid-air, the horse has already committed where the foot will touch the ground. However, before the foot leaves the ground, the horse's mind is more open to being influenced to place the foot where we choose. Therefore a rider has a better chance of getting a horse to place the left fore to the left if we can time our use of the left rein just before the left foot leaves the ground.

If the rider is late with the timing of the left rein the horse will already be committed to landing the foot in front and we'll have to wait until the left foot is about to leave the ground next time before trying again.

Good timing is widely considered a key element to good horsemanship because it clarifies the purpose behind what we asked. Nevertheless, good timing is about intervening in the moment between thoughts that occupy a horse's mind, and does not coincide with the movement of the horse's feet. That would be reacting to a horse's response long after it has already made the decision to respond.

Poor timing is a hindrance to a horse's learning because it causes confusion by rewarding a horse after it has moved from the thought we want it to have to a new thought we didn't want.

Most of us have timing that lies in between good and poor because we wait to reward the horse after it has moved its feet, but before it changed to a different thought. That's something we should be all working to improve.

Timing: The Early Bird

Summary: *There is another aspect to timing, which involves the way we intervene to correct a horse. Horses are always talking to us with their body language about how they are feeling and what they are thinking. On most occasions when things go wrong, a horse has given us prior warning about how it feels and what it is thinking. The earlier we can interrupt those undesirable thoughts and feelings, the more likely it is we can help a horse maintain focus, be clear and find softness. Allowing things to worsen and deteriorate into full-blown trouble will make the job of rescuing the situation more difficult and damage the trust we are trying to build.*

Not only is timing about when to ask and when to stop asking something of a horse, but also about the timing of our intervention to correct something our horse is thinking of doing.

Most of us don't act on a problem until the problem is out of control. We don't see how things are shaping up in a way that will lead to a problem and fix it at that point. We only see and respond to issues that put us close to the edge of real trouble rather than at the first hint of trouble. We act after the event, instead of before it.

A while back I had a lesson with a long-time client. She wanted to work on helping her pony feel better when separated from other horses on a ride.

The pony was well educated, although in no way an advanced horse. An incredibly sensitive horse, it could be high-strung and reactive when it had an emotional meltdown. But it could also work off a thought and knew a lot about how to be a good riding horse. The result was that the pony could give a rider a fraction of its mental commitment and still do most of what was asked.

During the lesson I arranged for another horse to be tied up nearby. As the lesson proceeded, I pointed out a number of tell-tale signs of trouble my student was missing. There were moments of crookedness, moments when the rhythm changed slightly, moments when the pony's thought left the arena, etc. Most times these moments were fleeting and barely perceptible. Nevertheless, they were enough to tell me that my student was not getting more than a small percentage of the pony's focus.

As I pointed the signals, the student did a great job of addressing each issue as they arose. The clarity she offered her horse by being early was making a big dent in the horse's need to be with the other horse. It was not long before I could stop coaching her and let her work through the problems. After a few minutes there was a clear and obvious change in the level of focus and relaxation the pony offered.

At that point, the other horse was led away to test the quality of change the pony made. The horse showed a definite interest in the other horse's departure, but my student was early enough to intervene with her idea. The pony immediately returned its thoughts back to the job. I was very proud of both of them.

Addressing the earliest moment of deterioration in how a horse is feeling is a powerful tool to building a clear understanding with a horse. If you don't address the small issues while they are still small, you are left with trying to rescue your horse from a bad situation.

Sometimes you won't be able to rescue the horse and are left to bail out of an unsafe situation. Even if you can recover, your horse you may have lost some degree of trust in your leadership because you allowed it to enter into trouble. There are only so many times you can do that before a horse loses confidence in a person to keep it safe.

Feel

Summary: *Feel is a rider's awareness of both the inside and outside of a horse. It is a skill that people need to learn as a pre-requisite to being a good horse person. Like most things with horses, feel is not all or nothing. It's a continuum that begins when we are starting out with very little feel and builds as we evolve into better horse people. Feel is also a conversation between horse and rider. When a horse is offered a feel, it will respond back with a feel. Both the horse and the rider continue to exchange feel as part of any ongoing conversation that forms the basis of working together.*

To me, feel is the ability of a rider to be aware and interpret accurately what is happening both inside (mental state) and outside (physical state) a horse.

I don't think anybody can argue that feel is not essential in becoming a good horse person. Yet, some people talk about it as if it is a spiritual gift that only the chosen have. Many believe feel cannot be taught. I don't believe that is true. I have seen the results of good teachers helping good students to be aware of things about a horse that they didn't know existed up to that point. I remember a friend helping me, as a young rider, to be aware of the feel when a horse was ready for me to ask for a canter. It wasn't long before I was aware of the preparation a horse made before the canter transition.

Developing feel starts with thinking about all the input your senses pick up when you ride or handle a horse. Often we need somebody to make us aware of these things, especially if we have been ignoring them for many years. Most of us can feel when a horse is about to buck, but how many can feel when its breathing pattern changes or its eyes are blinking furiously? Can you feel when your horse's back relaxes? Can you feel which hind foot is about to move? Can you feel when your horse needs a break from the work? Can you feel the moment when its focus changes?

Feel is also a two-way form of communication. While we spend countless hours working at developing a better feel of our horses, we often ignore the importance of offering our horses a better feel from us. By that, I mean when we present our aids, energy, movement, pressure, etc, to a horse, how does it feel to the inside and outside of that horse? Do we offer these things in a way that is comforting and clear, or in a way that bothers a horse and leaves it confused? The feel we offer a horse is a significant determinant in the clarity with which we communicate our intent. It's not possible to be completely clear without offering a good level of feel to a horse.

I like to watch people working horses. I particularly like to watch people working young horses. I am interested in watching what they offer a horse rather than what they can make a horse do. Some people have better feel than others. Other people are very effective at getting a horse to do things, but don't offer too much feel to the horse.

The people with good feel are good at reading what a horse is thinking and feeling, and figuring out the reasons a horse does what it is doing. They know the limits and boundaries. What makes them particularly good horse people is they know how knowing this information can help them present an idea to a horse in a manner that best fits the horse.

It's not enough that you know your horse is feeling something. You need to learn how to offer a horse a feel, so that it can offer a feel back to you. It's a reciprocal communication. If you are not feeling what your horse is presenting, you have nothing to offer back that it can follow or take an interest in. It's like the rider is talking about the state of the economy and the horse is talking about the cute chestnut in the other paddock.

I think part of the reason so many people have problems with their horse's focus is that they don't offer a feel to a horse that has meaning to it. When you present an idea to a horse in a way that does not take into account what the horse is thinking and feeling, a horse has no reason to take an interest and be attentive. Eventually, this can become a habit that you have to live with for a very long time. When a horse has developed the habit of not being attentive you can say goodbye to your dreams of being in a true partnership, because the only thing that will get its attention now is a lot of shouting and strong energy.

A feel that has meaning can be something large, small or in-between. It's not defined by the magnitude of what is being felt. A feel that has meaning to a horse is a feel that causes it to want to listen and encourage it to try to figure out what is being said. Again we are talking about communication that runs both ways.

You may have heard the expression "getting with your horse". When you get with your horse, you are also trying to get your horse to be with you. It's the same as offering your horse a feel and receiving a feel back from your horse.

When a person is learning to offer a horse a feel, I think it is often best to start with small things. Things like picking up a horse's feet, lining alongside a fence or moving one foot at a time are good exercises for people to work on offering a horse a feel. You can do these things without feel, too, by trying to make them happen. If you take your time and focus on the little things, it won't be long before you and your horse are having a secret conversation that only the both of you know is happening. It is too subtle for outsiders to see, despite the importance or signifi-cance it has for you and your horse. This becomes the foundation for building a true partnership based on the feel each presents to the other.

Understanding Feel

Summary: *The study of feel in training is mostly left to horse people, because science does not yet have the tools to equip it to understand feel in context. While humans express themselves with words, horses do it through body language. It is the feel of body language that allows horses to express themselves. The context of the feel is what gives meaning to a horse's intent. While skilled horse people can read the feel in context, science is not yet sophisticated enough to do this.*

I was involved in a discussion about the science of training versus the feel of training. On one side of the debate was the argument that science explains or will explain what feel is and how to use it to obtain the best outcome. The other side believed that feel is beyond the ability of science to describe, decipher and manipulate.

The pro-equitation science group became quite heated that the anti-equitation science group were so intransigent in their view.

Let me say that I don't know if science will ever be able to account for feel in horse training. They can't do it at the moment, and I am not sure if they will ever be able to do it. Equitation science is in its infancy, and I believe you can equate its present development in understanding horses and training as comparable to the way Galileo understood the universe versus our present knowledge and understanding; it has a very basic and primitive understanding.

In fact, I think most good horse people have a clearer and more accurate comprehension of how horses operate than equitation science does. I believe the working of the equine mind and how horses operate is vastly more complex than any of us realize.

I believe science (especially behavourists) approach the study of the horse as if it were a machine with some quirky habits. In a nutshell, they seem to take the stance that all horses can be programmed to behave in the way humans want, if it is approached with the correct language and in a scientific and disciplined manner. This notion may change in decades to come. The study of horse behaviour and training may eventually become more sophisticated, but right now it is quite primitive in my opinion.

On the other hand, many people with the opposing views assign the concept of feel to something mystical, spiritual and extremely elusive. They often make it out to be something that is almost unachievable to nearly everybody except the few people with a special gift. I don't believe this is true. I believe everybody has feel at some level. If you have a good relationship with a person or animal, then you have feel.

I think the hardest part of having good feel is not in presenting it to a horse, but in listening to the feel the horse presents to us.

Humans are talkers. Our primary form of communication is through speech and writing. Words are our tools of choice when it comes to presenting ideas, directing movement and expressing emotion. If a horse were to think about how humans communicate with words, they would probably think it is a mystical and spiritual form of language.

But with horses it's different. They emote through body language. To a horse, feel is so easy and obvious; it's like breathing to them. Sounds make up only the tiniest fraction of a horse's communication options. And they are hopeless at interpreting sounds and turning them into action. When you teach a horse to trot at hearing the word 'trot', it may give you a trot, but the only trot you get is the trot it offers. You can't tell a horse to try 'extended trot', 'working trot' or 'collected trot'. It's not within a horse's ability to decipher complex sounds and turn them into complex actions. When we talk to horses, it's mostly just babble to them.

Furthermore, horses are incapable of interpreting the meaning of a sound in context. For example, when we say the words 'meet' and 'meat' they will have the exact same meaning to a horse irrespective of the context we use. But humans know precisely how to place different meaning to the words by how we use them in the context of a sentence.

Yet when it comes to body language, a horse can differentiate between subtle changes such as the energy when we approach a horse in anger versus when we approach it in a welcoming fashion. A horse can't differentiate between sounds by their context, but it can differentiate between body language or feel by its context.

However, when horses talk through body language and feel, it is mostly just babble to us because our brains are more highly tuned to words. We notice the big changes in body language, just as a horse may hear the word 'trot'. But we don't understand the subtle forms of body language, just as a horse doesn't understand the words 'collected trot'.

We are really poor at interpreting the different meaning of body language and putting it in context. For example, many people can't distinguish the difference when a horse licks and chews because it is relaxed or processing a thought or is highly stressed. We tend to just assume licking and chewing has one single meaning. But it doesn't. It has different meanings depending on the context. Likewise, a horse with half closed eyes could be stressed or relaxed or shut down. A horse that yawns could be displaying stress or relaxation. The meanings of these behaviours all depend on the context.

So a horse can't separate the meaning of the words 'meet' and 'meat' and a human is poor at separate the meaning of a relaxed yawn and stressed yawn.

My point is that the hardest part of feel is feeling the language of the horse, and not simply presenting our intent to a horse through feel. We generally have more trouble reading feel than we do offering feel. We are pretty good at having our say, but not listening to horses having their say.

This is why the science has such a long way to go before it becomes useful to the training process. It has not yet developed the tools to analyze and decipher the feel or body language of the horse in context. On the other hand, good horse people are much better at this. People may not hear everything a horse has to say, but we keep trying and our degree of deafness is diminishing as we learn.

Working with horses inevitably involves a two-way communication between horse and human. There is constant discussion. Even when you think a horse is doing nothing, he is talking. It takes considerable feel to be good at hearing the stream of discussion coming from our horses and requires thousands of hours of working with horse to develop. Most of what horses express is beyond the sophistication of present scientific methodology to observe. But one day that may change.

Balance

Summary: *Balance is the amount we do between doing too much and too little. When we ask too little of a horse we teach it to ignore us and we are doing little more than nagging our horses. This can create considerable anxiety in a horse. Conversely, we are punishing a horse when we do more than necessary to evoke a change of thought. Punishment is never a tool for learning.*

In my view, balance is incorporated within the concept of feel, but it is separate. So balance and feel are the same, but different. This may take a little time to get your head around because comprehending concepts that are interwoven, yet separate can be challenging.

In my discussions with people, I find they are often referring to balance in terms of physical balance where the body is working equally both forward/backwards and side to side. That is, does a person have a centre of gravity that causes them to neither lean forward or back or left or right? That seems to be what most riders are thinking when they talk about balance.

To me, balance refers to the ability to find the middle ground with a horse. By middle ground, I mean the space between too much and too little. For example, if asking a horse to have forward motion I need to balance the pressure I use between asking too much with my seat and legs where the horse wants to run away from me, and asking too little where my seat and legs are ineffective in changing a horse's thought.

It's the balance between making a horse feel troubled and it not being aware I asked anything of it. It's the balance between having its thought on you and directing its thought to be somewhere. It's the balance between a horse looking at something and a horse mentally leaving.

There is a balance in everything we ask of a horse and in everything we offer horse.

It doesn't matter what aspect of riding or training or horsemanship we have in mind, to me balance refers to the Goldilocks syndrome of feeling what is too much, what is too little, and what is just right.

I think this middle ground is very important in training and riding and not often discussed or as widely appreciated, as it deserves. I say that because when we do too little to get a change in our horse, we become an annoyance and a stress in its life. Very often it learns to shut us out of its thinking and it's hard to get a horse's attention back.

When we do too much, we also become a source of worry to our horse. In order to motivate a change of thought in our horse, we need to help it discover that its present response to our suggestion is less comfortable than the response we want it to offer. This requires adding an eye drop of anxiety into the old behaviour that we want to change. If it only requires a drop of worry to motivate our horse to search for a new behaviour, yet we load it up with a bucket of worry, we create just as big a problem as if we did too little.

Any time you use more pressure than is required to motivate a change in a horse, you are punishing the horse. There is no teaching in punishment and there is no learning in being punished. There is only the fear of being punished. So balance becomes the middle ground between being irrelevant to your horse and punishing your horse. Balance is the spot where confusion gives way to clarity.

Consistency

Summary: *I believe being highly consistent is extremely important in bringing clarity to a horse. Even with mediocre timing, if a person is very consistent in their presentation and their reward, a horse will still eventually find clarity in the work. However, I don't think the opposite is true. A person can't be effective if their timing is brilliant, but their consistency is poor. We are most clear when we have good timing and a high degree of consistency.*

In my experience, most people talk about timing as being the most essential element to being clear in our training. I am going to challenge this accepted dogma just a little bit.

I don't disagree at all that timing is important when working with a horse. I think it goes a long way towards being better communicators with our horses, but I think the concept of consistency is not given enough consideration. I believe consistency in the way we present things to a horse is possibly the most important element to being good with horses.

I once worked on a property and used to feed in the morning and evening. I was not always consistent at what time the horses were fed. It could vary for up to two hours from day to day, depending on what horses needed to be worked. The feed room had a door that squeaked when it was opened. The noise of the feed room door being opened could be heard all over the property. It was far away from where the horses were kept and they did not know whether somebody was going in or out of the feed room. They didn't know the squeaking noise was from the feed room.

It consistently took about twenty minutes from the time I opened the door of the feed room, to the time I appeared with the feed bucket at the gate in a horse's paddock. When a horse first arrived, they saw me appear at their gate with a bucket and would come over to investigate what I had brought. Within seven to ten days every horse learned to go to his or her gate when they heard the squeak, even though there was a twenty-minute delay before the food appeared. This was a very consistent pattern despite the fact that I fed at different times of the day, and despite the horses not being aware the squeak was coming from the feed room and despite a twenty-minute delay between the noise of the door and the feed appearing.

If you were riding a horse and took twenty minutes before rewarding for doing the right thing, you'd be right to think you had really bad timing. I'm not suggesting you try that experiment because it wouldn't work under normal training circumstances.

Nevertheless, my point is that a horse can still learn in situations where the timing is poor, but the consistency is high. In fact, if a horse does not try different options while it is waiting for you to release the pressure, timing is probably not important at all. This explains the feed room door observation. Once the horses heard the sound of the door opening, their primary thought turned to feeding time and it did not change in the twenty minutes it took for the food to appear. In this case, timing was virtually irrelevant in teaching the horses to come to the gate. Timing is only effective if you offer a reward before a horse tries the next response on its list of options.

One of the biggest obstacles to being very consistent when we work with a horse is our own laziness; lacking the vigilance a horse requires from us. We are really good at letting ourselves off the hook when we are tired, or things get a little hard. People attend clinics or have lessons with an instructor and work really hard at doing everything they are told. They go home feeling much better about the path they are on. Then at home, when nobody is yelling at them or telling them what to do, they fall into the old habits of just getting by.

If people were more vigilant and self-motivated, progress would be quicker, easier, and they'd save money on not needing so many lessons and clinics. Our lack of attentiveness in being consistent gets on the way of progress with our horses.

Pressure

Before discussing the use of pressure in horse training, I think it is appropriate to have a brief discussion regarding the two major approaches that make up cognitive training in the horse world.

The most common and traditional approach is to use negative reinforcement techniques, but in more recent years positive reinforcement methods have gained some popularity. Positive reinforcement has developed from its use in the training of species such as sea mammals (dolphins, seals, etc), where negative reinforcement is not possible. However, positive reinforcement methods have gone on to be used widely in dog training and more lately in the horse world.

This book is focused on the principle of training horses using negative reinforcement techniques. The following discussion is a brief summary explaining why I choose to use this approach for most of my training. If you have an interest in exploring positive reinforcement training, there is a large volume of written and video material available on the subject.

Negative Versus Positive Reinforcement

Summary: *Most horses are trained using negative reinforcement techniques, however there are a number of people who prefer to use positive reinforcement methods. For the most part, people who rely on the use of positive reinforcement do so because they view it as a kinder form of training. However, this is not true for several important reasons.*

Most horse training utilizes the principles of negative reinforcement, however, a significant proportion of horse people incorporate the principles of positive reinforcement into their training. For those that might be wondering why these methods are not discussed in this book and why I generally do not use them in my work, I will give my thoughts on negative versus positive reinforcement methods.

However, first I should define the difference.

Negative reinforcement occurs when a stimulus or motivator is applied before a desired behaviour occurs in order to induce a behaviour. The stimulus is then removed when the behaviour occurs. For example, to ask a horse to walk, a rider's leg is applied to the sides of the horse as a stimulus, and then removed when the horse walks. The removal of the stimulus (rider's leg) encourages the horse to repeat the behaviour the next time the rider's leg is applied.

Positive reinforcement occurs when a motivator is given after a desired behaviour has occurred. For instance, a horse learns to be bridled by giving it a food reward after it opens its mouth to accept the bit. The application of the motivator (food) encourages the horse to repeat the behaviour the next time the horse is presented with the bit.

The most common form of positive reinforcement is called clicker training. It involves a marker of time (such as the sound of a clicker) to indicate to a horse that it has done something right. The horse is taught to associate that the sound of the clicker means a reward (usually food) will immediately follow. When a horse displays a desired behaviour, the trainer makes a clicking sound, followed by a morsel of food.

Firstly, I think everybody can agree that negative reinforcement is how horses operate in nature. In their natural habitat and among the herd, they learn the rules of survival through the trial and error of negative reinforcement. A horse does not establish its place in the herd by offering treats and hugs to the horses that do the right thing. Positive reinforcement is not something horses are naturally wired to understand. It is a completely foreign paradigm to a horse. Whereas, negative reinforcement makes use of a means of learning that horses are born knowing.

With that in mind, horses do not see the use of pressure and negative reinforcement as risky business. They view it as a normal part of both learning from others and of teaching others. If this were not the case, they would never form bonds. Yet, we know horses form very strong bonds – even with other horses that regularly set limits with pressure and negative reinforcement.

I feel I have a very good relationship with my horses. However, I am certain that if a building was on fire, my gelding Riley would run in to save my mare Six, before he tried to save me. Yet, Six is always telling Riley what to do and where to go like an old fishwife. The rules of their relationship are established and maintained constantly through the application of negative reinforcement without causing it any damage.

So in my view, it is wrong to assume that pressure and negative reinforcement are problematic to a horse or cause damage to the relationship one can have with a horse.

My point is that just because a horse experiences pressure does not mean a horse feels badly about it. I believe this is a central premise of good horsemanship that will be discussed in detail later.

The notion that the use of pressure and negative reinforcement are a way of 'forcing' a behaviour on a horse seems very common among the advocates of positive reinforcement methods. I think many people use this belief as a way of justifying the foreign concept of positive reinforcement in their minds. However, it should be clear that when done well, negative reinforcement is not designed to force behaviour on a horse.

Generally, those that criticize negative reinforcement are not thinking like a horse. It becomes about how people feel and not how horses feel. It seems that because humans think they would much rather be offered rewards and enticements for doing something, then horses must like positive reinforcement and hate negative reinforcement. Yet horses don't operate in this way.

Using pressure to inspire a horse to search for a different behaviour is not force in itself. Force only comes into training when a horse's options are whittled down to only one. As long as a horse is free to explore multiple options and choose for itself which behaviour is in its best interest, then force is not an issue.

Of course, there are many that use pressure and negative reinforcement incorrectly and do actually try to impose their will on a horse by ever increasing pressure. This is where the use of gadgets and techniques designed to dominate a horse come into play.

Nevertheless, I think the concept that negative reinforcement is a bad thing is misguided. Horses understand it and use it daily in their own lives, and when done properly it offers horses focus and clarity that lead to a good relationship.

What about positive reinforcement? Is it misguided?

One of the most rationalized justifications for using positive reinforcement is that it is kinder to a horse. This is not necessarily true. You only have to look at the many videos on showing clicker training to see very unhappy horses to be convinced that positive reinforcement is not innately kinder or that it makes for a happier horse.

The biggest cause of unhappy horses that are in positive reinforcement programs is the almost universal use of food treats. The use of food as a reward is a very strong motivator for a horse. Most clicker-trained horses become very focused on the treat and what they have to do to get it. At each stage of clicker training, in order to progress to the next stage, the food reward is withheld until the horse tries a new behaviour that the trainer desires. The withholding of the treat causes enormous stress in most horses. I have seen horses do some very bizarre behaviours in desperate hope that something they do will result in a food treat.

The second cause of stress in horses trained using positive reinforcement is the lack of clarity that accompanies the technique.

In the process of withholding a food reward in order to inspire a horse to search for a new behaviour, horses are largely left without guidance as to what the behaviour should be. Many trainers, who use positive reinforcement methods, leave it entirely up to the horse to accidentally stumble onto a response that results in a reward.

I think Australian trainer, Ian Leighton put it very well when he said, "Horses really like treats, so we are going to make sure they know we have treats, and that they may get a treat, but we are not going to help them understand what it is they have to do to get the treat.

"They have to work that out for themselves, because if we try to help them, that would be force. If they are either lucky or psychic, they will get a treat, but if they act confused and do other things they won't get a treat. I think a little empathy might be in order."

On the other hand, some trainers who use positive reinforcement do use pressure and negative reinforcement to some extent. They see it as an essential element of the process of using positive reinforcement. For example, in the process of teaching a horse to stop on cue using positive reinforcement, it also becomes necessary to make not stopping more difficult. So in their criticism of negative reinforcement they often forget to mention its importance in their work with positive reinforcement.

Lastly, I want to briefly mention gentle or kind training. I will discuss this in more depth much later in the book, but it is relevant to this discussion. As I said, many people choose to use positive reinforcement because they incorrectly believe it is a gentler, kinder approach to training.

In my view there is no such thing as training that is kind or gentle; they all create some degree of stress in the beginning. This is because in order to give a horse a reason to change what they are thinking and doing, the thing they are currently thinking and doing needs to be less comfortable.

In positive reinforcement training, withholding the reward or food treat causes the discomfort. The withholding creates a stress in a horse because the horse is seeking a treat. It is only by creating this stress that a horse searches for some other behaviour, which may cause the person to give them a treat.

The threshold level of stress needed for a horse to metaphorically say to itself, "this is no longer working for me. I had better try something else", is the same no matter which method you use. It may be different from horse to horse, because a sensitive horse may only need a fraction of imposed stress that a stoic horse might need to achieve the same threshold of stress. Nevertheless, for each horse, the amount of discomfort or stress will be the same, irrespective of whether you use negative reinforcement or positive reinforcement.

However, an important difference between the two approaches (and a large part of why I don't encourage positive reinforcement techniques when alternative methods are available) is that with negative reinforcement, the trainer can control the level of stress by adjusting the pressure they apply. In contrast, with positive reinforcement the level of stress is determined by how desperately the horse desires the treat, and a trainer has no control over that. So it is much more difficult to control the stress level with positive reinforcement to ensure that horse only experiences the threshold amount of stress.

This is a very important difference between the two approaches, because it means that very often, positive reinforcement results in horses that are far more stressed than would occur if the trainer had used negative reinforcement principles.

Pressure: A Part Of Life

Summary: *The purpose of pressure is to motivate a horse to search for a way to eliminate the pressure from its life. Horses experience both mental and physical pressure every day in normal life.*

When training horses, I almost always I use the principles of negative reinforcement in my work. The majority of horse people around the world practice this approach, so it is appropriate to discuss its role in bringing clarity to our training.

In this section, I will also discuss pressure in terms of the elements of timing, feel, balance and consistency in the context of how we apply and remove pressure. It is these ingredients that give clarity to the use of pressure.

It is important at this point that I make it absolutely clear what I mean by pressure because for many people the word 'pressure' has negative connotations and conjures up thoughts of abuse. This is not what I mean by pressure. Pressure is nothing more than a tool to encourage a horse to search to do something different.

In human terms, on a hot day the sun applies pressure for you to search for some action that will give relief from the heat. You might eat an ice cream, put on a hat, have a swim or go indoors. The sun provides enough pressure to motivate you to try something that will give relief. Yet, it does not cause you grief.

You don't hate or fear the sun. That is because the sun provides just enough pressure to coax you into a different behaviour and the answer is both easy to find and doesn't cause any stress.

Pressure is part of a horse's everyday life, whether or not humans are involved. They use pressure to move each other around. The sun beats down on them to create pressure for a horse to search for shade. The rain pressures them to turn their rear ends into the wind. Lice pressure them to search for a tree to use as a scratching post. A horse is always under some degree of pressure that inspires or triggers a response. The objective of the response is to escape the pressure. We should not be afraid of using pressure in our training, because horses understand it.

In order to be able to talk about how we use pressure to bring clarity to our training, I need to break it down into several factors.

The pressure we apply does not teach a horse to do something. It's the removal of the pressure that creates the moment of clarity to a horse as to what it needs to do in order to get rid of the pressure. Pressure is purely intended to cause a horse a level of discomfort that inspires it to try doing something different.

If I poke you in the chest with my finger, it will inspire you to find a way to stop the poking. If you move away and I stop, I have trained you to move when I poke you. But if you move away and I keep poking you, you might punch me in the nose, which would cause me to stop poking. Now I have taught you to punch me in the nose when I poke you in the chest.

Using Pressure With Feel

Summary: *The application of pressure is nothing more than the use of energy. However, the application of pressure with feel is the use of energy with clarity. There is a way of presenting pressure to a horse that is clear because it has feel behind it. Without feel, applying pressure can be very confusing and troubling to a horse.*

A long time ago, I was watching a student working her horse on the end of the lead rope. There seemed to be a disconnection between what she was trying to do and what the horse was trying to do. I don't think the horse was deliberately evading her, but it was obvious that at some level they were both speaking a different language.

As the session progressed, the volume of conversation between the horse and the owner was increasing, like two drivers arguing which one had the right to the only car space left.

As I kept watching, it was clear that the horse figured the owner was talking gibberish. It made no sense to the horse why she was bumping and wriggling the lead rope like it was caught in a tumble dryer. The horse pinned its ears, tossed its head and screwed its body into contorted shapes to express its confusion.

The owner was also feeling frustrated. To her credit, her frustration was with herself. She could see the trouble in her horse. She could see how cranky it was becoming, and she didn't know what she was doing wrong.

Only minutes beforehand she had watched me working her horse. It seemed to her she was doing the same thing she had seen me do. Why was the horse not behaving for her in the same way it had behaved for me? Was it the chaps? The hat? The beard? The gender?

After giving her some time to work it out I stepped in again to offer her some help.

I asked her to hold one end of the lead rope in both hands on her chest and close her eyes. I took the other end of the rope in my hand. Then I did my best impression of what I felt she was doing with the lead rope. The woman opened her eyes and gave me a blank look as if to ask, "What on earth was I doing?" Next, I used the lead rope like I was presenting an idea to a horse. Her expression completely softened and her eyes widened as if an epiphany had dawned on her. I can't remember the last time I saw such a clear-cut expression of the penny dropping.

The demonstration made it clear to her that what she thought she was doing and what she was actually doing were vastly different.

Even more important than that, she realized in a mechanical sense she and I were using the lead rope in very similar ways. She really wasn't so far off the mark. The direction and energy that her arm put along that rope was similar to the way I used the rope, but what was oceans apart was the feel that I presented along the rope compared to the feel she presented. There was a very small, but significant distinction that made the difference between the horse becoming more agitated and confused, and the horse becoming clearer, more confident and less anxious.

Everybody learns about feel in almost every aspect of life. You learn about applying pressure with feel when driving a car or hitting a tennis ball or pushing a shopping trolley. So I knew the owner could learn to offer her horse pressure with feel too, if she knew what it felt like to be the horse on the end of the lead rope.

The purpose of using feel in our application of pressure is to offer horses clarity of ideas. It is much more than simply applying pressure in a direction and with 'x' amount of energy – like pointing a finger and saying to a horse it should go over there (wherever 'there' may be). Feel changes everything in a relationship with a horse because of the clarity that energy with good feel presents. It clears up the confusion that is a barrier to a better relationship.

How Much Pressure Should We Use?

Summary: *In order to get a change in a horse, you need to be at least as strong as the strength of the thought that already occupies their mind. A horse's thoughts are always changing and the importance of those thoughts to a horse is always changing, too. That means we should always adjust the pressure we apply to accommodate the shifts in a horse's thoughts.*

"How much pressure should I use?" is an often-asked question. The answer is very simple: we should use the least amount of pressure necessary to evoke a change of thought. As the adage goes, "Do as little as you can, but as much as you have to."

So how much is needed to evoke a change of thought? The answer is even simpler. Since the biggest hurdle to re-directing what a horse is thinking is to eliminate the thought that is already occupying its mind, the amount of pressure needs to be at least as strong as the thought a horse has.

How strong is a thought? That's where a rider's feel is required.

Lear Jet (LJ) is a retired, aging Thoroughbred gelding and the herd boss. He takes the job of controlling the mares very seriously. Every winter he loses weight and I need to supplement his grazing with two feeds a day. In order to do this, I put him in a makeshift yard in a corner of the paddock while he eats, and then let him back with his mares when the bucket is empty.

When this first began, LJ would frantically pace the taped fence of his yard if the mares wandered to the far end of the paddock. When he had eaten his meal and I opened the gate to the yard, LJ would barge through the gate and gallop at high speed back to his mares. I saw this as a problem and decided to address it.

When LJ had finished eating I fitted him with a halter with a lead rope and did some ground work before opening the gate. On the first day, LJ had an extreme degree of focus on the mares. His thought to return to the harem was so strong that several times it took almost all the energy I could muster to get him to focus on me. On day two, his fixation became less single-minded, and I was able to guide his thoughts using much less pressure. By the third day I was able to open the gate and direct his thought without headgear. When I released him he calmly walked the 300 metres to join the mares as if he was going for a Sunday stroll.

This episode illustrated that the amount of pressure needed to create a change of thought is dependent on the strength of the thought already occupying a horse's mind. At first a lot of pressure was required from me in order to motivate LJ to forget about the mares and focus on me. As his emotions became quieter and the urgency to be with the mares diminished, much less pressure was needed.

I want to point out that the pressure I used was not to physically stop LJ from leaving to be with the mares, but to address the distraction they caused him. The importance of the mares in LJ's thoughts determined how much pressure I needed to apply to cause him to change his thought and stay mentally connected to me.

Using Too Much Pressure

Summary: *When you ask a horse to do something using more pressure than is required, it automatically creates anxiety in a horse. If this is repeated enough times, it leads to a horse having a flight response any time we present even a small amount of pressure. We should always be looking to use the least amount of pressure needed to encourage a horse to change its thought. Any more than that only hinders a good relationship with a horse.*

What happens if a rider overdoes the pressure and gets too strong?

I believe problems are created when using too much pressure. Beginning with too much pressure creates more anxiety in a horse than is required to get it to search for an answer. This can have the effect of causing a horse's survival instinct to kick in and his mind is filled with hard thoughts.

When this happens, a horse's brain switches from trying to think its way out of trouble to automatically trying any means of escape that might save its life. A horse stops thinking and starts reacting, which gets in the way of the lesson we want it to learn. Responses turn to reactions. Flooding a horse's brain with too much pressure can overwhelm it.

Imagine your first day at a new job and the boss asks you to make a hundred copies of a memo using a photocopier you have no idea how to work. It's stressful enough when he asks you to use a machine you don't even know how to turn on, but what do you feel when he stands over you and shouts that he needs them done in two minutes or you are fired? Suddenly you find yourself desperately pushing buttons hoping it will work.

A good example of this is when a person asks their horse to circle around them on the lunge and swing the tail end of their lead rope or flick a whip at the horse's hindquarters to get them started. So often, the horse jumps or flees forward to avoid the pressure. It feels worried by the pressure and goes into escape mode to avoid it. In extreme cases, it can cause a horse to try to kick, rear or strike at us to defend itself from what it sees as a life-threatening situation.

When you ask with more pressure than is required to direct a horse's mind, you are needlessly punishing the horse. Instead of presenting yourself in a way that provides calmness and clarity to a horse, your actions are punitive and muddy the meaning of your intent leading to a lack of clarity and confusion.

By applying more pressure than just enough, you run the risk of waking up a horse's survival mechanism because it fears its safety is threatened. When a horse feels its survival is in jeopardy, it is loath to let the worry and tension dissipate. Every time you ask the same question of your horse you'll get a heightened level of tension, which can show up as rushing, stiffness, freezing or even dangerous behaviours such as bucking or striking.

It is always a good idea to begin asking a horse with less pressure than you think you'll need because even if you are wrong, you can always increase the pressure and no harm is done. However, if you begin with more pressure than was needed, you can't take it back. The ill feelings it created inside the horse can't be undone. So start with the least amount of pressure you think will register to your horse's brain and you reduce the risk of doing too much.

Using Too Little Pressure

Summary: *Nagging a horse by using too little pressure creates just as much confusion and lack of clarity as using too much pressure. It's important that we do as little as possible, but not so little that we become ineffective.*

In my experience, when people use too little pressure it is an attempt to keep their horse quiet and relaxed. They want to use methods that are gentle and don't upset a horse, so they err on the side of doing too little rather than doing too much that might distress their horse. However, in my view 'enough' pressure is the smallest amount of pressure needed to motivate a horse to search for an answer. Therefore, if we do less than that, our horse will not search. It will mentally and physically continue along the same path despite our efforts to get it to change.

Any time we ask a horse to make a change and we don't get a change we are training our horse to ignore the pressure. In human terms, we are nagging our horses.

By taking away that niggling, ineffective pressure without some sort of change in what a horse is thinking, we are teaching them that our presentation has no clarity. To a horse, pressure that is insufficient to motivate it to change a thought is still troubling. In my view, this can sometimes be as much a stress to a horse as imposing too much pressure. Both approaches will interfere with our horse's clarity and damage our relationship.

Teaching A Horse The Importance Of Pressure

Summary: *When a horse has become dull to pressure, we need to re-educate the mind to become more responsive to less pressure. We start by asking first with the least amount pressure possible. If there is no response, the pressure should be increased sufficiently to teach a horse the importance of the least amount of pressure.*

Most horses that have little experience with people are highly sensitive to pressure. They are often more trainable than horses with a bad history of training. It's sometime said that training a horse to do something well the first time is easier than re-training later in life. This is because bad habits have not been instilled in the mind of the younger horse that need to be overcome in the older horse.

When a horse is learning an exercise for the first time, it has no idea what the correct response to pressure should be. Horses are not born with an innate knowledge how to respond when a rider applies pressure. The correct response has to be introduced into the mind of a horse at the stage the horse is ready.

I said previously that the purpose of pressure is to motivate a horse to search. So when starting a horse under saddle and wanting to teach it to go forward from my legs, I apply the minimum amount of pressure to encourage it to think about what it needs to do to eliminate the pressure. As long as the horse is searching, the pressure does not have to change. If the horse became reactive to leg pressure, I would decrease the energy of my legs. If the horse ignored the contact of my legs, I would increase the pressure until it began to look for something to do.

I can't overemphasize the importance of this principle. When a horse is searching, there is no need to increase the pressure. Just wait until it tries something close to what you had in mind, and then remove the pressure.

What about an older horse that has been taught to ignore small amounts of pressure? How might you use pressure to re-educate it to give meaning to subtle amounts of pressure? It makes sense that with better education we should be able to do less for a horse to give more.

With a horse that has been taught to ignore small amounts of pressure, it's going to take a lot more to get it to change its mind about small amounts of pressure. A horse that has been taught to tune out to subtle degrees of pressure will not search for a better response until the level of pressure is stronger.

A general guide is to always begin with the amount of pressure you would want your horse to respond to. This should be done even if you are certain it will not motivate your horse to search for an answer. If your horse ignores your light request, then it would be appropriate to follow with a firm enough pressure to induce a try in your horse. By doing that, the horse will begin to think it important to search when you first ask with a light pressure.

At the risk of repeating myself, I want to point out that increasing the pressure is intended to coax a horse to search for a new way to respond and have a change of thought, not to impose a new response on it. So even if a horse does not offer the exact response you hoped for, a try is a try and should be rewarded.

The Release Of Pressure

Summary: *Arguably, the most significant component of using pressure is knowing when and how to offer a horse relief from pressure. When we offer a horse a relief from pressure, there is a quality to the release that can make a difference to the learning process, and therefore offer better clarity. It's important to consider whether or not to release pressure completely or only partially, and how much time should elapse between releasing for one task and asking for the next.*

Horses learn by the release of pressure. Like pressure itself, a release is not always all or nothing. There can be degrees of release, where we offer a horse a reduction but not a complete absence of pressure. Sometimes the release should be small and incremental, and others times it should be a complete removal of pressure.

How do you know how big a release of pressure to offer a horse in order to maximize a horse's understanding?

Well, there are no golden rules about these things, and much of it comes down to your best judgment. I generally consider the amount of release should be proportionate to the amount of try and/or struggle a horse is experiencing. If a horse was working hard to figure something out, I would offer it a big release when it made a good try. Other times a horse may be fussing around the edges of trying to search for an answer, in which case perhaps small releases are appropriate for small tries.

Then there are times when the pressure we offer a horse has caused a horse a large emotional turmoil. We may have created such strong emotional trouble inside a horse that it is unable to think or search for an answer. In such cases, it may be best to offer a complete release (or close to) of pressure, even when the try from the horse is very small. This is because a horse's ability to search for answers is overwhelmed by the stress and anxiety it feels by the situation. A horse can't wear its thinking cap when it is swamped by fear and worry. Giving the horse a complete break from the pressure can help it find calm to the extent of being able to search through the problem once again.

The other aspect of releasing pressure that should be considered is how much time should elapse between releasing pressure for one thing before applying pressure for the next thing. I believe this is a different consideration to the timing of applying pressure or releasing pressure that was discussed in the section on Timing.

It's a tough question and I don't have a definitive answer. I think it comes down to once again, using your best judgment because it is going to vary from horse to horse and moment to moment.

I believe the amount of time between offering a horse a release of pressure and then asking for something again, can be very important in the training process.

I also think the appropriate amount of time will vary depending on the emotional state of the horse. A horse that is emotionally settled probably needs less time for the understanding to sink in than an emotionally charged horse.

I think many highly-strung horses learn best when there is a clear and distinct 'let down' time between jobs. In fact, I have experienced many times that if I am struggling to get a change in an anxious horse, that leaving it for another time can make a huge difference to how the horse responds the next time I repeat the exercise. I think breaking the pattern of the roller coaster of emotions that some horses experience when struggling with pressure makes more of a beneficial difference than spending hours battling, trying to get a change.

There are some horses where going from one form of pressure to another form of pressure can be a release for a horse, too. Again, I am generalizing and reminding you that it varies for each horse and each situation.

As an example, when backing a horse using the reins, you might continue to ask for a back-up until you get a softer moment. As the reins are released, you might use your legs to direct the horse immediately forward. In essence, you did release the reins, but in a practical sense you merely substituted one form of pressure for another with no time for zero pressure. There was no 'let down' time. The horse went from one job to another and one thought to another with different pressures. Yet, this can also be a release for some horses from which they can learn to soften to the reins. This is a grey area, and I caution you about it. Many trainers who use flooding techniques adopt this approach as a way of life when working with horses.

Each horse is different and each moment is different for each horse. How we offer a horse relief from pressure will impact on how well a horse learns the lesson. It requires a great deal of awareness and feel to present the best type of release to ensure our message is as clear as possible to a horse.

Releasing Pressure With Feel

Summary: *In our attempt to have good timing in our release of pressure, we sometimes suddenly remove the pressure and leave a horse with nothing to feel between horse and human. This abandonment of connection can encourage a horse to lose mental contact with the rider or handler and break the line of communication, leading to confusion.*

I notice time and again that many people have the habit of releasing pressure from a horse by abandoning the horse. It's most obvious when we look at the use of the reins, so I am going to refer mainly to how this relates to releasing rein pressure. Nevertheless, this discussion is equally relevant to the release of pressure from a handler's body language, rider's leg, a whip, lead rope – in fact any device or manner with which pressure is applied to a horse.

So what do I mean by 'abandoning the horse'?

A human example might be when we are having a conversation with a person and we suddenly turn to answer the telephone. The person we were conversing with feels abandoned and unsure what to do next.

When we are training and apply a feel to the reins, we wait for the horse to yield to that pressure. In our attempt and enthusiasm to reward the try, we often just open our hands and suddenly drop the reins as if we were holding something very hot. We try to mark that moment when we feel them make a try by instantly dropping the feel in the reins. In our effort to have good timing, we abruptly release the pressure the instant we detect a change, but we sometimes create a different set of problems when we do that.

By releasing the pressure so hastily, the reins are not there to offer a horse anything to feel. They are gone, and the lack of something to feel can allow a horse's mind to quickly wander away. The horse's only choice is all or nothing when it comes to following the feel of the rein and what the rider is presenting. In this case, the horse is either yielding to the rein or it is mentally somewhere else. There is not much room for anything else.

I'd like to think that my horse would not mentally wander away from me just because I released the pressure, and appreciate that the release of the reins indicated that it 'got it'. I don't want the next thing I ask from him to be an interruption to its thought, now drifted away.

It is so common for people to drop the feel when releasing pressure, that the problem of horses feeling abandoned verges on being an epidemic in my view. It is important that people give more thought to how they offer a release, because the quality of the release teaches a horse so much about our intention.

An easy method that goes far towards avoiding this problem is to remove the pressure more gradually, so there is a constant feel connecting the rider with the horse's mind. I would like my horse to be always checking in with me to see what might be asked at any moment, and by keeping the connection, I can help it try to stay with me.

It is possible to maintain a feel between horse and human without a horse feeling there is pressure.

Can Pressure Be A Comfort To A Horse?

Summary: *When a horse is confused by the work, our aim is to apply pressure in a way that presents clarity to a horse. Horses seek the comfort associated with clarity. So* *when pressure contributes to less confusion, a horse can find solace from pressure.*

Most people think of pressure as causing stress in a horse, and this is true to an extent in the early learning stages. The stress comes from a horse not knowing how to respond to remove the pressure. It doesn't come from the pressure itself. If a horse were clear in understanding what it needs to do to eliminate the pressure, the stress would be minimized. Furthermore, a horse can gain comfort from pressure where the purpose is clear, because it gives the horse clarity and predictability as to what is expected from it.

So many people go out of their way to creep around a horse because they know the horse will get upset if the pressure is increased. Rather than avoid using the right amount of pressure to eradicate confusion, we should find ways that help a horse to find clarity and comfort from the pressure.

I think there is no clearer example of this than in how a horse learns from a paddock fence. If a horse is in a paddock bounded by plain strands of wire and wants to graze on the other side of the fence, it will push against the fence and try to get its head under the lowest strand. The fence is a partial barrier, but it is a fuzzy barrier. It does not cause the horse to change its thought. There is nothing to stop the horse trying to get the grass on the other side; the fence just makes it more difficult.

This difficulty is a frustration and causes the horse stress. It doesn't ever totally give up the idea that if it could push a little harder or a little longer it would be able to eat more grass on the other side. The temptation to lean on the fence to get a little more grass plagues the horse's thoughts. As I mentioned earlier, pressure that it is too little to cause a horse to change a thought does create a significant stress in a horse's life.

However, imagine the horse was moved to a paddock that was bounded by an electric fence. After the initial shocking discovery that the wire is electrified, a horse stops trying to push on the fence to get to the grass. It quickly learns that touching the fence causes a lot of discomfort. It also learns that there is no danger unless it touches the fence. The fence does not reach out and grab the horse.

When a horse is clear about how an electric fence operates, the fence does not pose any worry and the horse gives up the thought to try to reach the grass. A horse can fall asleep with its nose a few centimeters from the electric fence and feel unconcerned because of the clarity that the fence creates in a horse's mind. Thoughts of trying to reach for a little extra grass on the other side no longer frustrate the horse.

A few years ago I broke in a filly that was really sensitive and easily upset if the pressure was more than a whisper. Her flight instinct was secondary to her instinct to fight. When you increase the pressure, most horses fear response is to run away. However, this horse would immediately go into battle and lose the ability to search for an alternative answer.

Luckily I picked up on this very early and tried to present every new thing to her in tiny steps and with patience. She was quick to learn as long as the pressure never got too big.

Over the following weeks, her confidence grew. Bit by bit, she could handle more pressure and became more capable of calming down after a fright. Eventually the filly viewed pressure quite differently than she did when she first arrived. Even with a huge amount of pressure, she looked to me to see what was the problem.

One day, I was leading her from the paddock and a mob of kangaroos bounded down the hill straight towards us. The filly got a fright and tried to pull away. I told her to stay with me, but her fear blocked out anything I had to say.

I then had an explosion of my own, big enough to wake the dead. Instead of scaring her further, my explosion calmed her. She remembered I was still there and that felt okay to her. The sudden appearance of the kangaroos was not nearly as important as she first thought. I was proud of her.

I can never protect a horse from stress and worry. It is part of everyday life. But what I hope is that, as a horse's training moves further along, the pressure from the human becomes more of a comfort than a worry. If I firm up with a horse, I want it to look at me and think, "Okay, what went wrong and how do I fix it?"

Firming up with a horse is aimed at inspiring clarity, not fear. As a horse understands that more and more, it won't worry about the pressure we present, but view it as something to take away the anxiety. It can be a comfort to a horse in its moments of confusion.

Of course, as a horse progresses in its education, you hope that applying more pressure is something that will become less necessary. There will always be times when a horse loses focus and feels unsure of the proper response. Sometimes this might entail being really firm with a horse, but if the relationship and the training are right, this should not cause the horse to go into survival mode with inappropriate behaviours of flight, fight or freeze.

The Role Of Using Flooding Pressure In Training

Summary: *Flooding is the practice of applying pressure to a horse without relief until a horse stops resisting. It can cause a horse to feel helpless and resistance is futile, leading to a horse becoming shut down, yet obedient.*

Flooding is the process of presenting a pressure or stressor to a horse that is not removed until the fear response is diminished.

It is commonly seen when most people desensitize or sack out horses, where exposure to something fearful is maintained until a horse stops trying to flee the object.

Two things are required for flooding methods to work. The first is you need something that bothers or stresses a horse. It could be anything from a rider's leg to clippers to travelling in a trailer. It doesn't matter what it is. The second thing is to restrict the horse's ability to escape the stressor. A horse can't be allowed to escape the thing that worries it. In flooding, the only way a horse finds relief is to give up fleeing or fighting. In most cases this leads to a horse shutting down and accepting its fate.

It is rare that the use of flooding leads to good feelings in a horse because the very nature of the method takes away a horse's opportunity to make a choice. Flooding imposes behaviours on a horse, and does not allow it to choose a response that it feels is in its best interest. For this reason, you'll hardly ever see a horse that feels comfortable in its work when flooding methods have dominated the training.

Flooding, as a technique, is extremely common and you might be surprised to find that something you do or a highly-regarded trainer does, can be counted as flooding. For example, driving a horse in a yard to create 'join-up' or 'hooking-on' is flooding a horse with pressure until the flight response is diminished and the submissive drive is awakened. People get excited because their horse turned to come into them. Yet, horses really have few choices because all other ideas resulted in being driven even more. The fence of the yard prevents escape from the pressure and the driving does not stop until the horse quits running and turns in.

Another example would be to tie a horse to a post and allow it to pull back until it stops. This is such a common method of teaching horses to tie-up that people forget the principle behind the method is to teach the horse the futility of expressing an opinion.

However, occasionally flooding does not lead to submission, but aggression. There are a few horses that appear to have missed out on inheriting the genes for submission because they will fight the training to the point of disaster. I remember attending a horse-starting clinic by a well-known trainer. There was a horse that was saddled for the first time and did not find the feel of the girth very comfortable. When it exploded, it was scary.

In fact, the horse was so reactive that nobody could get near it to remove the saddle at the end of the day. It was left in the yard all night having to wear the saddle. I wasn't present the next day to see how they finally got it off. Even so, that horse did not respond well to the girth pressure and flooding in this case caused the opposite reaction to what the trainer was attempting. Who knows what psychological damage flooding did to that horse?

There is no doubt that flooding is part of every trainer's methods. There are some things (like the first time a horse is girthed) where flooding cannot be avoided, and is even useful. Just the practice of dropping a lead rope over a horse's back over and over can be a form of flooding in the beginning.

Nevertheless, there are ways to make adjustments to the way a stress is presented to a horse that better prepares them and brings clarity to the training. For example, before girthing a saddle for the first time, a person can prepare a horse using a belly rope or by walking beside the horse and using their hand to snug a rope or girth against the horse's belly and then release – using an approach and release method.

However, I believe too many people make flooding the mainstay of their approach to training. I think it is because it is easy and it is quick.

Not a lot of skill is required to teach a horse to submit using flooding methods. You don't have to be brilliant with your timing, feel and balance to get results. And you can forget about focus, clarity and softness; they are largely irrelevant when it comes to applying flooding methods. To use flooding as a training tool, a person just needs to recognize submission (or lack of it) for it to work.

Flooding is also generally a quick method for horses that are prone to submission. It may not be quick for horses that will argue their point until the end, but those horses are few. You won't come across many horses in a lifetime that will fight to the end.

So flooding is a way of getting a rapid change in a horse. However, it should be remembered that the change is only on the surface and does not go deep inside a horse. This is because flooding generally does not create clarity and softness; only obedience. And when obedience is no longer enough, you don't have a lot to work with.

I am going to put this out there and I'm ready for the negative feedback, but every 3 or 4-day colt-starting clinic I have seen (and there have been many) involves predominantly flooding methods. Some trainers are very talented at using it, others not so talented. But they all exploit the nature of a horse to submit to flooding techniques in order to get them ridden and compliant in a very short time. That is a large reason why I believe no horse that goes home from a colt-starting clinic is really broken-in.

It is only what goes on at home after the clinic, that determines how the horse turns out. The clinic only gets them submissive enough to allow somebody to sit on them, and walk, trot and canter. But that's the easy part of starting horses. The hard part is to get them feeling okay and directing their thoughts, and I've never seen that at a 3-day starting clinic.

People are often impressed with the power of flooding to create a well-behaved, quiet horse. However, it is easy to confuse a horse that has given up the fight to become submissive and obedient, with one that looks to be happy and have a good relationship with its rider.

Desensitization

Summary: *I know a lot of trainers spend time using desensitizing techniques. However, if a horse is shutting out the world as a coping mechanism, then the horse can't prepare for the next thing that is about to be asked. Using pressure to desensitize a horse in a traditional sense destroys the clarity that pressure and release are meant to bring. I view methods like this counter-productive because they often create problems in the future.*

When I was a kid, most of the time when people talked about desensitizing a horse, they were talking about sacking out. This involved constantly exposing a horse to something that scared it into an early grave until the horse got used to it. Often horses were tied up or hobbled to inhibit their flight response, and then flooded with whatever scared them. The flooding would only desist when the horse stopped trying to flee or avoid the stressor.

All horses experience a form of desensitization at some point in their life. For example, saddling a horse for the first time involves tying down a hunk of leather onto its back, which stays there until the horse is calm enough for the trainer to be able to get it off again. There are lots of other examples such as fitting a rug (blanket) for the first time, being locked into a racing barrier or being caught in a fence. I have known a few people who make a practice of tying horses to a tree for hours at a time, letting them struggle until they give up.

For many people, desensitization or sacking out involves making a horse stand still while cracking a stock whip around them or throwing tarpaulins over them or even lunging them with bags of plastic bottles tied to the saddle or surcingle. These are all flooding techniques designed to kill the flight response inside a horse.

I want to be clear that the flight response cannot be killed. It can be severely dampened, but because it is an integral part of a horse's survival instinct it can never be eradicated. The need to survive is arguably the strongest instinct a horse has – possibly stronger than the need to herd or eat or reproduce.

Any attempt to eradicate the flight response in a horse is futile because there will always be something that brings it to the surface. It's not possible to expose a horse to everything that it feels might jeopardize its survival. There is always the possibility that something new will trigger the need for a horse to run for its life.

As trainers, we have two choices about how we approach desensitizing horses. The first is to flood a horse with scary objects until they learn to ignore them.

The second approach is to teach a horse not to ignore the object, but instead learn that it will not threaten their safety. On the surface these two approaches probably seem like the same objective, but they are not.

Teaching a horse to ignore something that worries it is fraught with trouble. In my opinion, if we continue to expose a horse to something that it feels might get it killed, we are basically telling the horse that we don't care if it lives or dies. The horse is learning that we can be the source of the trouble because we put it in danger. It's not possible to have a good relationship with a horse or have a horse that tries if it considers it can't trust us to not jeopardize its safety.

The alternative approach is to teach a horse that what scares it is not so scary after all. This can only be done if we ensure it does not try to tune out the scary object. We require the horse to deal with it and explore it rather than pretend it does not exist. In order to do this I will use an 'approach and retreat' method to help a horse overcome its fear. That is, I introduce the scary object gradually to a horse to the point where its awareness and worry become heightened, then remove the object to allow the horse to feel safe once again. I would repeat this process until the horse feels incrementally better and safer, and where it is no longer bothered by the object.

However, I need to be sure that the horse's lack of flight response is not because it is tuning out the object. So I need to test if the horse is ignoring the object or just feeling okay about it. I might do this by using the object in such a way that I ask the horse to move in response to it. If the horse yields to pressure from the object, but does not flee from it, I can be confident that my horse is both aware and feeling okay.

For instance, if my horse is scared of plastic tarpaulins, I might use approach and retreat techniques to help my horse not feel the need to run when I introduce and eventually rub it with the tarpaulin. Interspersed with that, I might also flap the tarpaulin or tap my horse's back with it to ask it to move around me. Then return to rubbing the horse with the tarpaulin.

When I can rub my horse with the tarpaulin and also direct my horse in response to it without the horse feeling worried, then I know my horse has learned a valuable lesson about pressure and clarity.

Obedience Versus Willingness

Summary: *The role of clarity in good horsemanship is to create a willing horse rather than just an obedient horse. When obedience is prioritized at the expense of a horse's emotional welfare, we severely hamper what a horse is capable of giving to the relationship and the work.*

Most forms of horsemanship are designed to teach obedience to a horse. That is, a horse does what it is told, when it is told, and how it is told. When a horse is not obedient, the pressure is steadily increased until it submits.

I believe in most cases, obedience comes from a horse's fear of the consequences of not being obedient. In contrast, obedience in good horsemanship stems from a horse's confidence that a rider's idea is a good idea. I prefer to call this willingness.

How can teaching obedience without willingness be avoided?

It comes down to the priority we give to our clarity. Do we give more importance to what a horse is doing, or to what it is feeling and thinking?

I believe a horse has the right to say "No" to us - particularly if it is convinced that saying "No" will save its life. It would be stupid of me to point a gun at another person and then get mad at them for running away.

On the surface, training obedience can appear similar to training willingness. While they may look as though they are the same, the outcome is usually very different. The thing that is missing from an obedient horse, but present in a willing horse, is choice. In good horsemanship, we strive to give a horse options to choose its preferred response. We might slightly skew things in favour of the choices we would like a horse to make, but we don't make the other options unthinkable.

If we make the option we want a horse to choose just a little less horrible than the alternatives, we really haven't offered a horse a choice it can feel comfortable about. No matter what option it chooses, they are all bad; it's just that one is less bad than the others.

For example, I know a trainer that took on a horse that had a problem with weaving its head back and forth in the yard. It would do it all day. The trainer put a halter on the horse and attached four or five strings to the halter that had one-inch bolts tied to each end. Any time the horse moved its head, it was hit in the face by the swinging bolts. The horse's choices were narrowed to two; either stand still, or move and be hit in the head. Neither choice felt good to the horse.

This is how we make a horse slavishly obedient rather than happily obedient. In good horsemanship, we want a horse to feel no concern about the choices we ask it to make, not just marginally less concerned.

I think liberty training is a good example where some people believe obedience is paramount. Liberty horsemanship, where horses are ridden or worked with no gear attached, can be seen at virtually every horse exposition, performed by a dozen or so different trainers. Many people consider a horse being worked with no gear is an example of the highest quality of horsemanship. However, in some cases, the training it has taken to enable a horse to perform at liberty can leave a horse feeling just as trapped, and with no choice to express its true feelings, as if it was being worked with the most severe equipment available.

In good horsemanship, obedience alone is not enough. This is because if you are working with a horse that only understands to do what it's told, you'll find the horse will only offer the bare minimum in effort. A horse's try will be about doing the least amount to keep it out of trouble.

This has two limiting consequences. The first is a horse will hold back from doing the very best it can. The second is that once a horse comes across a situation that causes it more worry than the worry of not being obedient, you have nothing to work with. If crossing a rickety bridge troubles your horse more than a crack of your whip over its hind end, then you might as well go home for the day.

In my opinion, the reason why obedience has become the main focus of most people's training is that it is easy. Horses by their nature are very submissive, so with only a little talent, most people can train obedience into a horse. If they can't, there are tack stores filled wall-to-wall with gadgets that will help them teach it.

So much of horse training is about making the horse do something in the hope that it will learn to feel okay later. However, most times it is a matter of a horse resigning itself to a situation, rather than finding comfort. This results in many unhappy horses doing what they are told.

In every discipline of equestrian sport, people talk about the quality of a horse's movement or the execution of a certain maneuver. In dressage, reining, western pleasure, etc, competitors are scored according to the quality of the movements. Governing bodies like the Fédération Equestre Internationale pay lip service to the idea of the 'happy horse', but make no real attempt to ensure that riders with unhappy horses aren't rewarded with blue ribbons or gold medals.

As a result, people have come to assume that the focus of training needs to be on the obedience of the feet. When they do this, they forget that the horse's feet are controlled by the horse's mind.

Most horsemanship is the art of training the unwilling to become obedient. Good horsemanship is the art of training the unwilling to become willing

The Shut Down Horse

Summary: *When a horse shuts down it becomes mentally disconnected from what is going on around it. I believe it comes from a person's attempt to instill obedience in a horse where it feels that expressing opinions or feelings about the work is futile and the horse feels helpless.*

As an extension of the idea of the role that clarity plays in producing obedient versus willing horses, this brings me to one of the long-term consequences when we make the training of obedience the most important priority.

During a clinic a few years ago the question was asked how does a horse become shut down? This is a question that I believe directly relates to clarity or a lack of clarity.

Firstly, what is a shut down horse? I consider a horse that is shut down to be fairly unresponsive, lacking in focus, exhibit an inability to take an interest in the person or what the person is presenting. In some horses (but not all), there is a propensity towards spontaneous explosive behaviour.

I also believe all horses are shut down to some degree. It is a feature of a horse's nature that makes them submissive and able to be trained. The best children's ponies are often very shut down in order to cope with a child's lack of feel, timing and clarity. But even well trained horses show some level of being shut down in some aspect of their work. It is an extremely common phenomenon.

I think that shutting down is a coping strategy used by horses in circumstances where things feel unsafe or unclear to them and they feel a sense of helplessness and futility in complaining or fighting. They see no way out of the trouble, so they shut down.

Horses don't begin life being shut down. It is a learned strategy that develops where a horse is forced to accept things as its lot in life and arguing about it is pointless. They mentally hide and avoid engaging in things that trouble them. Going with the flow is the path that offers the least amount of trouble, but the try in a horse is killed or at least damaged.

So how does a horse become shut down? I think it comes about by two related mistakes that people make.

The first is that people try to impose a response on a horse, as I discussed in the previous section.

The second mistake I think people make is overly criticizing a horse. Humans are very good at telling a horse it got it wrong or made a mistake. We tell it "No" every time the horse does something we don't want. When we say "No", we often don't help a horse find the thing we do want. I sometimes see examples of this where a horse is told "No you can't do that", then it tries something else only to be told "No, you can't do that", so it tries something else and once again is told "No, you can't do that". The criticism is constant and the pressure is relentless, yet the horse remains unclear as to what it can do.

Finally, it is important to recognize that when a horse shuts down with an impregnable resistance it is because it believes mentally excluding the outside world is a safe haven. Many horses will strongly fight being pressured to mentally and emotionally participate when they have already learned how bad it can be. When trying to help a horse come out of a shut down state, survival instincts can surface and a horse may exhibit dangerous behaviour in the process. It is definitely not a training job for a novice horse person.

As I said, I believe shutting down is common, but the better horse people work hard to avoid it and minimize it where possible. Some horses shut down to the extent that they would hardly raise an eyebrow if they stepped on a grenade during a trail ride, and in other cases, the shut down response is so small as to make it appear imperceptible to some people.

The Road To Clarity

Now that we have talked about some of the essential elements of clarity, how do these fit together to bring clarity to a horse during training?

I'm going to discuss some of the concepts I use in my own work to help my horses learn and understand the training lessons as clearly as possible. It should never be forgotten that within these ideas, I incorporate the fundamental elements that I have already discussed, in everything I do with a horse.

Without these principles, clarity is not possible; they are like the stitches that hold the suit together. If one stitch is missing the whole thing eventually unravels.

Where To Begin Working With A Horse

Summary: *Where does a person decide to begin the work with a horse? The simple answer is that you begin at the first point you see emotional trouble or resistance. At every step we should try to eliminate worry and anxiety in order to get a horse in a learning frame of mind. Therefore, wherever a horse displays concern, we begin by trying to relax its mind and improve its focus.*

During a clinic, I was asked, "When you have a horse that needs ten things fixed, how do you decide where to begin?"

Surprisingly, I couldn't remember ever being asked that question before. It was an excellent question and one I reckon most people ask themselves many times during their life with horses.

However, the answer is very simple and it never changes. It is always the same answer no matter what unwanted issues your horse has developed.

You begin with emotionally relaxing your horse.

I believe that as far as training is concerned, emotions drive behaviour. Bad emotions create resistances and poor behaviour. Good emotions promote soft responses and compliant behaviour. Anytime you experience resistance, agitation, mental distraction, sluggishness or reactive behaviour, you can be sure ill feelings are the root cause.

As we have all heard a million times, training for the day begins the moment you approach your horse to catch it and doesn't end until you've walked away at the end. A horse does not differentiate between when you are doing actual training and when you are just leading it somewhere. Each experience has implications for how a horse will feel and respond during the next experience.

With that in mind, in answering the question, you begin with how your horse feels when you approach to catch it.

That may sound too basic to matter, but let me tell you the overwhelming majority of people have no clue how their horse feels when being caught, haltered, led, saddled, etc. They incorrectly assume that just because their horse is easy to catch or walks up to greet them to be caught, that the horse feels good. This is not true for most horses, most of the time. Yet people are not aware of this.

This concept of checking how your horse feels, should continue throughout the entire process of working with a horse. At each step, it is important to do whatever can be done to eliminate as much tension and worry as possible. That might be in how it leads, to how it executes flying lead changes. It all matters. No resistance or worry is not important or should be ignored.

The reason that a horse's emotional comfort is so important is that without a calm and quiet mind, there can be no learning. There is no clarity. When a horse's mind is bouncing around looking for better ways of finding comfort and safety, there can be no room for learning the lessons we are trying to teach. It may succumb to obedience, but it cannot learn to let go of resistance.

A horse will struggle and argue in the training until the end of its days unless it feels emotionally comfortable and mentally quiet.

So to reiterate my answer to this very important question, each day begins with whatever it takes to help a horse become more emotionally comfortable. In training, there is no greater responsibility than to work at that.

Encouragement Versus Criticism

Summary: *Fostering the ability of a horse to search and try is linked to our ability to encourage a horse in the things we want, rather than discouragement through our criticism of the things we don't want.*

I want to expand on the notion of criticizing a horse that I mentioned briefly in the section on the Shut Down Horse. The way we approach correcting a horse's mistakes plays a big role in bringing clarity to our training.

In our attempt to make sure bad habits don't become in-grained, we are often constantly trying to correct the smallest mistakes. Yet the big danger we make in this style of training is that the horse feels relentlessly criticized.

As I have said earlier, when a horse considers its options are taken away, it is left feeling hopeless and helpless, partly shut down and afraid to try.

In other circumstances, sensitive horses may fear being criticized so much that they offer any response they can think of even before the rider has asked anything, in the hope they can avoid the pressure. They become hyper-reactive.

Most people are not guilty of over-criticizing their horses to the extreme, but nearly everybody does it to some extent. It is very difficult to avoid completely.

I think one of the big mistakes we occasionally make, which can lead to a horse feeling overly criticized, is when we get a change, we don't know what to do with. It seems that people observe that their horse suddenly has a change of thought for the better, but then are at a loss of what to do with that good response. Instead they carry on and wait for it to fall apart, where they can once again criticize and correct their horse.

They wasted the change their horse offered. Instead of putting that good change to work in a way that can make sense to a horse, they keep carrying on until they lose the change again. From a horse's point of view, there was no point in trying. We see the change as an end in itself rather than as a means of getting something better.

At a clinic I attended as a spectator, a trainer rode a horse for a woman. The horse was quite edgy and lacked focus. After the trainer rode the horse it was going really well. By the time he dismounted it was time to move onto the next lesson, but the trainer insisted the owner ride the horse in the car park while he went onto the next rider and then she was to return and tell him what she felt. I watched the owner riding her horse in the car park.

At first it looked great, but within a couple of minutes it was falling apart at a great rate of speed. I asked her what she thought was going on. She told me that at first she felt her horse was a different horse. It felt amazing. Then she said she didn't know what to do with how good he felt. She had spent a lot of time always telling her horse what it was not allowed to do and when that was no longer her project because of what the trainer had done, she didn't know what to do next with the horse.

The lack of leadership and guidance left the horse lost and confused, so her horse drifted back into old habits, and what it knew best.

This is a problem I see at clinics from time to time. Riders work so hard at fixing the little resistances and imperfections their horse displays, that when it changes, they have no idea what to do next. Both the rider and the horse are left floundering in a void.

I believe this can be avoided if a rider has a plan for what to ask next from a horse. Once a horse has made a change, mix it up, rather than keep working on the same thing. In addition, before asking for any change from a horse, it helps to bring clarity to have a plan with what to do with the change. Present a horse with a job that was made possible by the change.

For example, if a horse is rushing forward you might help it to relax and slow down, and then make use of the new relaxed state by perhaps asking for a leg yield into a corner. By asking for something else, a horse won't feel it is being drilled to death and it has a new job that utilizes the change the horse made. This can bring clarity to the things we ask.

The Role Of Repetition In Training

Summary: *Clarity can only be gained by repeating a lesson because each repetition reinforces an understanding in a horse's mind. The number of repetitions will depend on many factors that affect a horse's ability to retain a strong association between being asked for a response, and what that response should be. The negative side effect of repetition is the danger of drilling a horse to the point where clarity is replaced with confusion.*

It's probably stating the obvious to say that horses don't automatically perform an exercise correctly once and then know it for life. Exercises and responses are learned by a pattern of association. It's not from doing it once. It's from a pattern of doing it many times.

Various trainers have different opinions about how many times an exercise needs to be repeated before a horse has learned it. I have heard numbers from five to twenty-one times. In my view, the number of times you need to repeat an exercise correctly will depend on what you mean by having 'learned it', the individual nature of the horse, the consistency with which the trainer presents the exercise, the emotional state of the horse, and the focus of the horse.

Firstly, I think a person needs to define what they mean by a horse learning the correct response. How do you know when a horse has learned the lesson? Is it when it gets it right 100 percent of the time, 80 percent of the time, or less? Is it when a horse knows the exercise in the arena at home or when it can perform it in the middle of a new and stressful environment? Is it when a horse knows when you ask, or when someone asks who has never before touched a horse?

There are always limits to the declaration "my horse has learned it". The notion that 'a horse has learned it' is not definitive. How much an exercise needs to be repeated will depend on how you define the statement 'he has learned it'. Pablo Picasso once said about art, "A painting is never finished. It is just abandoned". I think this is a sentiment that could be applied to both horses and horse people, because horsemanship is a life-long process of learning and refining.

There is another aspect of learning and clarity that involves repeating an exercise, which has had me curious for many years. Despite thinking about it and experimenting with different scenarios, I still haven't developed a true understanding of this pattern, but it relates to the importance of repetition in a horse's learning.

I have noticed when a horse is struggling with how to respond correctly, it eventually hits on the right answer and immediately gets rewarded. Then when it is asked the same question again, the horse chooses a different answer to the one for which it was rewarded.

In fact, it is my experience that it takes three more repetitions of struggling to find the right idea before a horse once again hits upon the answer I am looking for. I don't know why three is the magical number, but I've observed this happen with the majority of horses. It doesn't matter about age, breed or history - it's nearly always the same. I estimate about 80 percent of horses offer one correct answer followed by three wrong answers followed by another correct answer, before they develop an association of what they are being asked to perform.

It has always been very curious to me about what is so magical about three wrong answers. Why not one right answer or twelve wrong answers? I can only put it down to the nature in the way a horse's brain operates.

Although repetition is a very powerful tool in bringing clarity to a horse, it can also be detrimental if overdone. We must be vigilant and aware of when to stop repeating an exercise. There comes a point in every lesson where the lesson becomes predictable or even boring. It's the point where the horse's focus starts to drift away. It is important that we don't go beyond this point. It's when repetition becomes drilling.

People drill their horse over and over because they are looking for perfection and not satisfied with improvement. Not only does drilling an exercise cause problems with a horse's focus, but it also makes a horse more confused because it cannot find a response that gives relief from the drilling.

A few years ago I was asked to help a woman whose horse was prone to suddenly bolting in the arena. She would be riding along with everything seemingly okay, then with little warning, the horse would spin and gallop as fast as it could to the other end and stop. I noticed that she had been picking on the horse to perfect its hindquarter yields. Over and over she asked for a hindquarter yield.

After the horse bolted and stopped in the corner of the arena, the owner immediately dismounted and asked if I would ride the horse.

I hopped in the saddle and instantly felt the horse's stress and reluctance to pay attention to me. I worked the horse like we were playing polo all by ourselves. We rode all over that arena with no discernible pattern or predictability.

When we got to the corner where the horse had tried to bolt earlier, I felt it shape up to leave to the other end. I quickly interrupted that thought and instantly continued on with our polo match. The horse never tried to bolt on me a second time and finished much softer in both its body and mind.

The horse was stressed by the owner's drilling of the hind-quarter exercises and I believe the bolting came from an expression of the futility it felt.

The role of repeating an exercise is to ensure a horse clearly understands the lesson. Once the lesson is reproducible it is important to move onto something else to avoid the damage that is done from mindlessly drilling a horse and keep a horse's mind engaged. You can always come back to the lesson a little later for refinement.

Nothing Comes From Nothing

Summary: *Every experience in a horse's life is a learning experience. The way a horse responds to a request from a trainer is largely determined by the lessons that came before. When there is a problem in the training, it is usually because the focus, clarity and softness of the previous lessons are not established enough for the new level of difficulty. Franz Mairinger once said, "There are no problems at the higher levels". I believe he meant that every problem that appears in the more advance levels stems from a problem in the basic level. It's important to re-trace the steps and fill in the gaps in the earlier work.*

Everything a horse learns is derived from something it learned before. Nothing ever comes from nothing. The clarity with which a horse learns a lesson is largely dependent on how well it learned the lessons that came before. They form the foundation to base progress in training.

For example, how a horse gives to pressure when we direct it to move in a round yard might be related and traced back to the day it was born and its mother moved it to suckle from one side to the other. Every experience the horse had with giving to pressure from the day it was born, to when it was halter broken, weaned, saddle broken, taught to trailer load, etc, had some impact on the way it yields to pressure today. Every experience is a learning experience.

This is a useful concept to keep in mind, because it means that every resistance we come across in a horse has a starting point. A horse offers resistance because a lesson that came before wasn't good enough. In order to overcome the resistance, it's helpful to go back to the spot where resistance started to creep in. If you can't find that spot, then go to the spot that the horse finds less troubling and build from there.

Training progresses in increments not leaps and bounds. Training is building layers upon layers of previously learned tasks. When you strike trouble, go back a step or two and establish more focus, better clarity and softer softness than you have. If you try to gloss over the lack of focus, clarity and softness and barge through the resistance, the problems will only become more obvious as the work gets harder and more demanding.

I believe that the secret to training at higher levels is no more than refining the basics of the meaning of the reins, legs and seat. The same meaning of the reins, legs and seat that we try to teach a horse when it first begins its career as a riding horse is the same meaning we continue to work on when we are performing at the Olympics. The only difference is in the refinement we have given the aids as our horse has progressed.

The same thing would be true for any discipline. If I was a reiner, teaching a horse to spin is just a refinement of teaching a turn. Teaching the slide is a refinement of the stop command. If I was a show jumping trainer, the only thing I need to train is the meaning of the reins, legs and seat. If I was a trick trainer, teaching a horse to perform circles around me at liberty or to rear on command or pick up objects in its mouth is just a refinement of the groundwork I have already taught my horse when I was halter training it. Trailer loading, tying up, catching, or standing quietly for the farrier are all just refinements of halter training.

Training may not be easy, but it is simple. When you hit a brick wall in your training program, instead of trying to blast your way through the resistance with more force and repetition, consider the option of going back a step or two and see if the meaning of your leg, seat and rein aids are solid enough for what you are asking of your horse. You should not move onto the next level of difficulty until you are sure you have the focus, responsiveness and softness to the aids that you are going to need for the next stage of training.

The Importance Of Leading Well

Summary: *Everything about a horse's mental state will be expressed in the way it leads. A horse's attitude with the work on a lead rope will be carried over into the riding. Owners sometimes underestimate the value of good groundwork as a means of improving the work under saddle.*

I can't over-emphasize the importance of having a horse lead well. The way your relationship starts, begins with the way you teach your horse to lead. If a horse does not lead well, things are not okay, no matter what advanced movements it is capable of in the arena.

It is my personal experience that most horses do not lead well. I find that surprising. It emphasizes the lack of importance people place on the quality of leading. A lot of people feel that as long as they can get their horse from the paddock to the saddling area without too much trouble, things are okay. Then they wonder why their horse won't pay attention to them when they ride. It begins with your relationship on the ground and for most of us that means how our horses lead.

I want to stress that the test for leading well is not that a horse follows without dragging on the end of the lead rope, or that it comes along with very little pressure on the headstall. That by itself is not an indicator of a horse leading well, because any horse can be taught to do those things on autopilot. Leading well also includes being able to direct a horse anywhere you like without stirring up bad feelings.

The ability to direct a horse with softness is a much more important indicator than a horse that can follow you around. You should be able to ask a horse to wait for you to go through a gate first, or you should be able to send it first and have it wait for you on the other side. You should be able to adjust a horse's position at any time with no feelings of trouble between the both of you. You should be able lead from in front, from the tail, from either side with no trouble. The list goes on and on.

The important thing is that your horse maintains focus and it causes it no emotional worry however you ask it to lead. These things are fundamental to getting the same feeling from a horse when you ride.

Many years ago I was trekking through the bush with a couple of my horses. I had an accident and suffered temporary blindness. My horse, China, was able to lead me to the creek twice a day for me to wash my eyes. I couldn't see where he was taking me. I couldn't negotiate the thick lantana bush or the log in the path – but he could. He led me. I didn't lead him. I didn't teach him to do this. It was only possible because he had learned how to feel of me when were together. I could not have relied on China if he didn't lead brilliantly.

People will come to clinics with a horse that is bouncing around on the end of the lead rope like a helium balloon on a windy day. When I ask them what they'd like to work on they inevitably say something like the canter or side-passing or shying or whatever – totally unaware that their problem begins with what is happening on the end of the lead rope while they are talking to me.

How a horse responds and feels on the lead rope tells a person a lot about the relationship they have with that horse. In my view, it's not possible for a horse to be the best it can be to ride and still be mediocre on the lead rope. Some horses are better to ride than they are to handle on the ground, but I am certain that if they were better on the lead rope, they would also be even better to ride. In a horse's mind, leading and riding are the same thing.

Training Versus Re-Training

Summary: *The concept of correcting bad training in a horse is the same as teaching a job for the first time. In both cases, the basic knowledge that a horse needs to have for the task is missing. So training and re-training are the same in principle.*

I am often reminded how people view horses with problems as being different from horses with no training. It is a very common perception that horses with training that we don't like, are different from horses that just haven't been taught in the first place.

All horses that have had any experience with people come with training. Even if they are foals that have not yet been haltered. They have an experience of people that leaves an impression on them. If they have only seen people from the other side of the fence, they have formed an opinion that has taught them something about humans.

If what they have learned about us is not what we want them to learn, they already have baggage that will impact on our relationship and how our training progresses.

My wife and I used to work with a lot of foals. Every year we handled a stack of them. Teaching them to pick up their feet and hold them quietly for the farrier was always on the list of things to do. We always started with getting them comfortable with having their feet touched, then progressed to getting them to shift their weight to the opposite leg and then having them lift their foot off the ground when we cued them. Pretty soon, they would quietly lift their leg and hold it up while we tapped their hoof and pretended to rasp around it.

At each step we ensured the horse was soft and feeling okay before moving onto the next phase. The job was not to make the foal lift his leg for the farrier. The job was for the foal to stay focused and soft for every part of the process. If we did that, the foal was automatically ready for the farrier.

I also remember working with an eight year old horse that was prone to kicking the farrier. The owner told me the horse was always bad about having its feet handled ever since they bought it as a broken-in three-year-old. Another trainer had used leg ropes to teach the horse to lift its leg and be shod. Even then it would fight, but they could eventually shoe the horse.

I started with getting the horse okay with me touching its leg and running my hand up and down it. When the horse became really good at the rubbing part, I rubbed its inside tendon. The instant the horse shifted weight to the opposite leg, I stopped. I kept this up until the horse just lifted its leg. I built on this approach until the horse could lift its legs and leave the hoof relaxed in my hand while I rubbed and tapped the leg and hoof and could put it softly back on the ground.

In other words, I re-trained the horse in exactly the same way my wife and I trained a foal to lift its leg for the first time.

Experience has taught me that in the majority of cases, re-training is the same process as training for the first time. This is because in both cases the problem is that the basics are either missing or have been corrupted, and allowed bad feelings to creep into the horse's emotions. Whether a horse has learned bad habits or just doesn't know how to respond, the solution lies in clarity of the basics. It's no different in my eyes.

Many times people have asked me about buying a young, untrained horse to avoid buying a horse that already has problems. I tell them that if they don't know enough to fix problems that already exist in a horse, then they don't know enough to ensure they don't put problems into a horse. The skills needed to train a green horse are the same skills needed to re-train a seasoned horse. People just need to go back to the beginning and fill in the holes that were left by the earlier training.

Good And Bad Sides

Summary: *Ensuring a horse is comfortable to be worked on the left and right is an important part of helping the horse become the best it can be. It can be advantageous to begin a lesson on the easiest side because often that will transfer some degree of clarity to the work on the harder side. It's often simpler for a horse to establish good changes on the easy side before trying it out on the harder side. There is no need to rush to work on the harder side until a horse has a better understanding of the training on the easier side.*

A few years ago I was stepping up into the saddle of a horse for the very first time in its life. The gelding was very nervous about having my foot reach up to the stirrup and even more nervous when I deliberately bumped his leg with my toe. The poor fellow was shaking all over.

I was working on his right side because I knew it was his better side. After I achieved a small change in the horse, the owner saw that I was quitting the session. She asked why I was not going to repeat the process on the left side. I told her that I would, but not today. This confused her because like most of us, she had been taught that you must always repeat an exercise on both sides.

I told her that the change the horse had made was only small and I felt it was not good enough for the horse to carry over any benefit to repeating the process on the left side today. It would be just as big a mess as it would if we had not done any work on the horse's good side.

There was no advantage to repeating the exercise on the left side at that time. And there was no harm in not repeating the exercise on the left side that day. When the horse makes a more significant improvement on the easy side, it would then be time to do it all over again on the harder side

I think that when you are going to start something that is a little bit challenging for a horse, it is best to begin on the side it finds less troubling. You don't have to. It's not a golden rule. Even so, hopefully a change for the better on the easier side will bring a degree of clarity and some assurance that the challenge is not quite as bad on the harder side. It's not always true that getting something okay on the easy side of a horse makes the harder side easier, but in enough cases, it can make it a worthwhile practice.

I'm all for getting both sides of the horse as good as possible. I believe the more even the horse is, the better horse it is. Even so, there is no urgency in working both sides in the same session, same day or same month, except in exceptional circumstances. If it's easier for a horse to have it put off until something else is cleared up first, then postpone it if you can. No harm will be done.

However, when the horse is ready to be able to handle the challenge on its hard side, don't postpone it any longer. There is no advantage in delaying the experience if a horse is ready.

When A Lesson Is Going From Bad To Worse

Summary: *When emotions are running high for a horse and a pattern keeps repeating itself, it can be a good idea to stop working and do nothing. This 'time-out' can allow calmness to return. There is not a lot to be gained by continuing on when a horse's emotional state blocks its ability to think and learn from the lesson.*

Sometimes we find ourselves in a battle of will with our horse. Despite our patience, and despite trying a different strategy, you'll have days where a small amount of anxiety turns into a meltdown. Sometimes it is because the horse is so overwhelmed by the stress of the situation that it stops thinking and keeps repeating the same pattern. The fear that we instilled can be too much for a horse to engage its brain, so it does what it has always done in a mindless fashion. In situations like this, it will not be possible for a horse to have learned the lesson we want until the emotions are quelled.

Whatever the cause, we have hit a brick wall and it's important that we recognize early the downhill slide of the horse's (and our own) mental state. There is no clarity to be gained by continuing on the same destructive path. The horse will stop learning, and to persevere with pushing through has the potential to cause mental and emotional damage.

In circumstances like this, it's a good idea to stop working. Stop the horse and stop yourself. Just bring all the pressure down to zero and have a quiet moment with the horse. You might even rub them gently or let them have a pick of grass or anything that will lower their emotional state (and yours).

Sometimes, just taking a break from the pressure of the job is enough to get a change in a horse. When you begin again they can often be in a much better mental spot and the try is more available to you. It is amazing how quickly progress can be made after resetting the emotional state of a horse to zero.

If this is not the case, then you could consider breaking the lesson into much smaller tasks. It's often a good idea (and never a mistake) to re-start the work with something you know the horse can do well. Choose a simple task and allow the horse to relish in the reward of getting it right. Then build from there in tiny increments, adding one layer of difficulty at a time, until you reach the lesson of the day. If at any time it starts to fall apart again, it is a good idea to go back a step or two to an exercise it could do easily. Then begin building up the layers again.

I also want to add that like horses, there is no place in a lesson for high levels of human emotion. If you feel yourself becoming upset, angry, depressed, despondent or even joyous, hold it inward. If you can't do that, take a break until it passes. Don't be demonstrative in expressing your emotions to your horse. They get in the way of your timing, feel and balance.

It's best to bury the dark emotions of anger or impatience until the session is over and your horse is put away. Even the good emotions like joy and exuberance are best left until there is at least a break in the work or the session is over. Human emotion gets in the way of our better judgment.

Do We Have To Finish On A Good Note?

Summary: *It is desirable to finish work on a good note, but it isn't essential. Sometimes you had better quit early before things go from bad to worse. The real problem with quitting before a horse feels better is that when it happens regularly, the horse learns to hold onto those bad feelings longer and longer.*

Most of us understand the concept of trying to ensure that at the end of a session with a horse, we leave it in a better spot than it was at the beginning. I have said myself at clinics that if you ask something of a horse you should make sure you get a change, otherwise you shouldn't have asked in the first place. To ask a horse to make a change and not get a change is teaching it to ignore what you ask.

Likewise, if a horse finishes a lesson no clearer than when it started, what's the point of the lesson? Not only will you not achieve an improvement, but you also run the risk of making things worse. There are very few horse people that will disagree with this idea.

As an overall good policy, I agree with it too, but I won't agree that it is a golden rule. I won't agree that leaving a horse no better or even worse off is a mortal sin. I won't agree that you 'must' always ensure a horse makes positive changes before the work is finished for the day. It is a good policy to do what you can to help a horse finish better than when it started, but I don't think it is a 'must'.

I know this goes against the accepted wisdom that many of you have probably heard over the years, but I will try to explain my viewpoint.

There are a few reasons why I don't believe it is vital that a session should only ever end when a horse has made a significant improvement.

The first is that any mistake or miscalculation or wrong path we make with a horse rarely leads to permanent damage. Horses are very forgiving and in most cases bad habits can be reversed. I have spent many years re-educating horses where owners have made mistakes, miscalculations or followed a wrong path for years before they sought help with their the horse. It may take more work, but it is rare that you can't teach an old horse new tricks.

If you finish today's work session with your horse feeling pretty bad, there is usually no reason why the positive changes you were hoping to make today can't be made tomorrow. We would all rather make sure we finish in a good spot, but there is no need to beat ourselves up if for some reason that doesn't happen. It can be fixed next time. Clarity made tomorrow is still clarity to a horse.

Another consideration is that with the training of most horses, there is a point that if you go past, a horse will stop learning. It just won't improve and can't recover because the horse has reached the limit of its capacity to focus. Mental, emotional and physical fatigue will start to weigh the horse down. The onus is on us to ensure we recognize when a horse is approaching this point and finish early even if it has not made the changes we hoped for.

It is potentially much worse to push beyond the point where a horse has had enough just because we believe we are not supposed to finish until it has reached a better spot than where it started.

Finally, now that I have told you it's okay to sometimes finish a lesson before your horse has made a good change, let me tell you that it is not okay if you do it all the time.

People often don't appreciate the effect a one hour session with a human can have on how a horse feels the other twenty-three hours of the day. It is my experience that if a horse is troubled in its work and is allowed to go back to the paddock carrying that internal trouble, day after day, eventually those troubled feelings remain with a horse much longer after the work has finished. Not only will it hinder a horse's improvement and get in the way of learning all the new cool stuff you are trying to teach it, but you also have a high risk of mentally screwing up a horse.

I compare it to a kid being bullied at school. The first day or two when the kid gets punched or humiliated, he shrugs it off by the time he goes home. But if it keeps happening each day, after a couple of weeks he becomes reluctant to go to school. After a month, he starts picking on his little sister. After three months, his grades have fallen, he is moody and sullen, argues with his parents and hardly ever leaves his room.

I've seen horses behave similarly. What was once a quiet, easy-going horse, no longer mixes with the other horses. They sometimes spontaneously gallop and buck around the paddock several times a day. They might bite at their sides. They pin their ears when being caught. They rip up their rugs (blankets) and chew on fence posts. The trouble inside them makes the other horses feel uneasy and the herd often ostracizes them.

It stems from the bad feelings carried from the work sessions back to the paddock, day after day. So it is important to not make a habit of leaving a horse feeling stressed each time we finish a training session.

Clarity When Training For Speed

Summary: *Teaching a horse to perform movements at speed with confidence and relaxation requires absolute clarity and confidence at slower speeds. It's important to go slowly enough to ensure a horse can be confident and relaxed at slow speeds before asking it to rush the movements.*

I see a lot of people working to put speed or snappiness into their horse's performance. It seems that when a horse moves fast and does a movement quickly there is a belief among some people that the horse is doing better. They equate lively movement with effort or try from a horse. Often times, horses competing in show jumping, barrel racing, reining, campdrafting and the like, are asked to perform at high speed long before that can perform well at slow speeds.

In my view, I think there is confusion between the concept of 'effort' and the concept of 'hurried'. There is no doubt that a horse that hurries through a maneuver is putting out quite a lot of effort, but a horse can make an effort without hurrying.

When you ask a horse to do something quickly, there is a natural tendency for a horse to have a surge of adrenaline. There is more urgency and tension associated with doing things rapidly. Most training that tries to instill speed comes from putting a worry in a horse. It involves having a horse flee from a driving pressure. It could be the whip, spur, bit, flag, or anything, but it almost always is the result of the horse's fear and need to escape from being driven.

So how can you get a horse to be quick without being fearful?

Having a horse that can work fast at the same time as being relaxed and confident is a long process. The answer lies in making sure a horse has clarity because clarity promotes confidence. You can only expect a relaxed effort when a horse has a clear understanding of the job and without emotional tension. This is best done at slow speeds where a horse is less stressed. If a horse carries even a small amount of worry at the slower speed, it will be magnified several-fold when you ask for the same job at a hurry.

So before you ask a horse to work at faster paces, you need to ensure that your horse is absolutely confident working at slower speeds. This doesn't happen too often, because a lot of people want to hurry the horse as soon as it knows an exercise. However, knowing the exercise is not the same as feeling confident in the exercise. When tension creeps into the work, slow down and wait until the horse can perform with relaxation and confidence.

The Clarity That Good Riding Brings

Summary: *I believe being a good rider has more to do with being an effective rider who causes a horse the least amount of bother and the greatest amount of clarity, than being a rider who sits correctly according to the established convention. A good rider will be clear in what they ask from a horse and not obstruct a horse in its job.*

For a long time I've been considering what is a good or bad rider? What makes one rider better than another?

Clearly, it's not just somebody who sits more correctly on a horse, although that can be part of it. There are lots of people who sit well on a horse and can still trouble their horses. It's not perfect balance or holding the reins correctly or not gripping with your legs or having the right amount of contact or no contact. All these factors can help, but there has to be more to it.

After some thought, I believe a good rider is one who is clear in the message they transmit to a horse's mind. A good rider does enough to plant a thought into the mind of a horse and the message is so clear and unconfused, that the horse immediately understands the message. A good rider brings clarity to a horse. I think this is what makes a rider effective and I believe horses prefer effective riders to correct ones.

My first mentor was a Dutch fellow who was nearly two metres tall and came from a show jumping family in Holland. He sat on a horse like a rag doll and sometimes his riding position was questionable. Nevertheless, he was one of the most effective riders I have ever seen. It didn't matter if he pointed a horse at a jump or asked for a half pass; he caused the horses minimum bother. It was a joy to watch how horses responded to him. He knew how to ask a horse, and then stay out of the its way so it could fulfill the request. Yet, most riding instructors would be horrified by how he sat a horse.

What made my Dutch friend an effective rider, are all the factors we have already discussed that contribute to clarity in our training. He displayed a degree of timing, feel, balance and consistency that minimized any confusion or ambiguity a horse experienced. And he rode with the intention to bring comfort and softness to the horse under him.

I think we all cause our horses some degree of trouble in our riding. We just can't be perfect all the time. When I say to people that I don't believe a horse can feel okay with bad riding, they often interpret that to mean they need to study correct riding position. And I would never discourage that, because I feel it is important that we all learn to sit in balance with a horse. However, if you really think about it, any riding that the horse can feel comfortable about must be okay, even if it means the rider is facing backwards and sitting on the rump.

There are good reasons why we have established guidelines about what is and is not correct about riding positions. We look at a rider and notice if he leans forward or backwards; or if his hands are too low or too high; or if he grips with his calves or not. We judge these things based on our understanding of the rules of a good riding position. I am not criticizing these rules because I understand that they were established to benefit the horse. However, our judgment is meaningless in the face of the horse's view.

If a rider fulfils all the requirements of sitting correctly on a horse, yet the horse is still bothered, then in my opinion they are not a good rider. I believe that unlike a textbook-perfect rider, a person who does not tick any of the boxes that define a correct riding position, but who can be effective and clear, while helping their horse feel okay inside, is the better rider.

Clarity Of The Reins

I would like to put the discussion about clarity in the context of the rider's aids. Specifically, I'm highlighting the reins because they are an example that is easy for most people to visualize. It is important that when reading the next few pages that you consider the concepts presented in the context of clarity for a horse.

Even though the discussion is confined to how to adapt using the reins to create clarity, the principles also apply in a general sense to the other aids. I hope it won't be difficult for people to transfer the concepts when thinking about a rider's seat and legs.

The Basic Function Of The Reins

Summary: *In their simplest role, the reins direct a horse's mind to influence the energy created by the rider's seat and legs.*

Reins can be a comfort to a horse because they bring clarity to its thoughts. Harry Whitney has said, "Between the reins lies a thought". It is our job to help a horse maintain its thought between those reins in a way that offers clarity and provides mental calmness and physical relaxation.

In my view, the most fundamental function of the reins is to direct the horse's thoughts. In the early stages of training, a rider's seat and legs direct the horse to have energy, and the reins tell the horse what to do with that energy. It's only when the horse is totally clear that the reins direct the movement through a change of thought, does a rider introduce the notion that the seat and legs can also direct the horse where to go. However when starting a horse, and for many months after, the seat and legs mean 'do something', and the reins tell it what that something should be.

That does not mean that my body is not passively encouraging a horse. It just means that it is not doing the bulk of the directing. So if I want to turn left, my body sets up for a left turn, with adjustments to my seat and legs to ensure I interfere as little as possible with the turn, but my left rein is doing the talking to the horse's brain. It's the same for forward, backing, stopping and lateral movement.

The most basic purpose of the reins is to communicate to the brain of the horse to direct its front end and its back end both independently of each other, and in unison. This is what I teach from the beginning, and something I try to ensure lasts a lifetime.

No matter how advanced a horse becomes, it should never lose the fundamental purpose of the reins. If you have a horse that works off the seat and legs of the rider, but their response to the reins is not so good, then you have a problem.

I begin teaching a horse the meaning of the reins from the ground. The first seed I plant into their minds is how to respond to the feel of the lead rope. A lead rope is nothing more than a rein, except the trainer is on the ground and not in the saddle. The same mental process that a horse undergoes to follow the feel of the reins happens first when learning to follow the feel of the lead rope.

The reason why it is so important in early training to instill clarity about the role of the reins, is that the reins offer the most direct means of offering very subtle corrections when a horse's thoughts stray. A rider's seat and legs don't offer the same level of finesse in the early stages. Having a horse soft and responsive on the reins makes the transition to teaching a horse to work from the seat and legs much easier in later training.

For example, when I begin teaching lateral movement to a horse I always start by using my legs and seat to ask for energy or movement. I do this using both legs at the same time. When I want my horse to move laterally, I only use the reins to direct the horse laterally. As long as it has energy to move, I don't use my legs to help the horse move sideways. If the energy dies away, I apply both legs simultaneously to get the life up again. However, it is only my reins that tell the horse's mind to think about moving sideways.

When it comes time to teach the horse to move sideways from my legs, it is a simple matter of applying my leg first, and a second later, use my reins to direct the horse away from my leg. My leg asks the horse to step sideways, but my reins reinforce the meaning of the leg. With repetition, the horse is side passing away from my leg without help from the reins. Most lateral movements can begin this way.

Uneven Feel In The Reins

Summary: *One of our goals in riding should be to have our horse equal on both sides, but this rarely happens. Horses are generally softer on one side than the other. The feel we present to a horse through our reins should reflect this difference. In order to address the issue we should adjust the feel in our reins to encourage the more resistant side to become softer. The resistance and softness between the left and right sides of a horse's body is dynamic and always changing. Therefore, contact of our reins should constantly change, too.*

A common issue that comes up at clinics is the notion of keeping the feel of the left and right reins even. Whether the reins should have an even amount of feel seems to cause confusion to many people.

As a young rider, serious about dressage, it was drummed into me by several instructors the importance of having an even contact on both reins at all times. I hear from students at clinics these days that this is still being taught as a golden rule.

As I developed as a rider and horseman, I discovered that an even feel on the reins was rarely a good thing. This idea is one of the things that puts me at odds with dressage riders attending my clinics. They struggle to see the problem with having the reins constantly even.

I believe having an equal feel on both reins is rarely a good thing, and most often it is counter-productive. This is because it is rare for a horse to be equally resistant or equally soft on its left side as its right side. Why would you present the reins in the same way to a horse's softer side as you would to the more resistant side?

The feel we put in each rein should reflect the difference in the resistance or softness on either side of a horse. It's a dynamic thing, because the resistance in the horse is constantly changing from side to side, moment to moment.

I am constantly working to have my horse equally soft on both reins. In the process of getting there, I am offering a different level of contact on the reins to match the different level of resistance my horse exhibits at any one moment.

Rein Contact

Summary: *Rein contact is the minimum amount of feel in the reins to evoke a change of thought. The purpose of contact is to provide clarity to a horse with the least amount of pressure and in the most effective way.*

Nowhere is the use of the reins more argued than in discussions of contact in the horse world. It's a topic of constant debate and ethereal concepts. The true meaning of rein contact seems to elude most riders and many trainers. So I feel it is an excellent topic for illustrating how the reins contribute to clarity in training.

Nuno Oliveira once said, "Contact is a private matter between the horse and the rider". I agree with this sentiment, because it emphasizes that only the person sitting in the saddle can truly determine the contact that a horse needs at any one moment.

The question, 'what is contact?' gets argued on dressage forums all over the world. It's one of the subjects that nearly everybody has a different opinion. Even many of the gurus of dressage can't agree. With that in mind, there is no chance that what I am going to say is going to sit well with everybody.

I think in order to understand what contact is, you must understand its purpose. Why do we want to have contact? If you can understand the purpose, you will be able to know when you have it or not, by how your horse responds. If you have correct contact you will get the result you want (or closer to it).

Contact is nothing more than communicating to a horse.

It is a means of conveying an idea from the rider/handler to the horse. You can have contact in the saddle and on the ground. You can have contact through your seat, your legs, your hands, your voice, your whip, etc. All these open a line of communication whereby you can convey your intent to a horse.

Now that we know what is the purpose of contact, we can then define it. When riders and coaches talk about contact, they are almost always referring to the feel on the reins.

Therefore, I believe correct contact is the minimum amount of feel on the reins required to evoke a change in a horse's thoughts.

The feel on the reins needed for correct contact is variable for different horses and at different moments for the same horse. Contact is not one thing. Since we are talking about the 'minimum' level of feel of the reins, contact will vary according to an individual horse's needs. On some very resistant horses it might be 10kg and on very responsive horses it might be the weight of a carbon atom. Both are correct for those horses. To ride a horse with a stronger feel on the reins than is needed is incorrect use of contact. Likewise, too little feel on the reins to help a horse change its thought is also incorrect.

The appropriate contact is never constant. It is always changing. It needs to change, because the availability of a horse's mind to listen to the contact always varies due to its shifting focus. The contact a rider might need to convey clarity to a horse may have to change in a moment-to-moment fashion in order for the horse to comprehend the message. The amount of feel you might need to apply to the reins will alter many times during a ride.

It's no different to being a teacher in a classroom. Sometimes the teacher can speak softly if the students are listening and other times they will have to shout in order to be heard.

In the world of dressage, horses are taught to 'seek' the contact. In other words, they are trained to push forward into the reins. In some horses, it is a simple holding of the bit at the end of the outstretched rein. In other horses it is a bearing down onto the bit - a leaning into the reins. It will differ a little from trainer to trainer. However, what dressage people almost universally criticize is to ride a horse on a rein where the only degree of feel is the weight of the rein; sometimes referred to as a slack or loose rein. It is widely considered to be incorrect, because they think that slack in the rein means no contact, no control, and a horse cannot work correctly.

Let's again look at the purpose of contact. It is a means of communicating a rider's intent to a horse and the correct contact is the minimum amount of rein pressure needed to evoke a change of thought in a horse. So, if riding a horse with a rein that is not taut can achieve both of these criteria, then the rider must be using the correct contact. In fact, I would argue that to ride such a horse with more rein pressure than that is incorrect contact.

The purpose of riding – any sort of riding – is to achieve as close to unity with a horse as possible. To me, this means that the means of communication we use to talk to our horse should be quieter as we approach that unity. The more advanced a horse becomes, the more subtle our aids, and the less pressure we need to convey our intent. It would seem that the ultimate goal of every rider would be to have a horse that can be directed by the smallest change and the least amount of pressure.

It therefore seems logical that a horse that can be ridden correctly with slack in the reins is more advanced than a horse that requires anything more than that in order to be correct.

I want to emphasize the importance of being ridden 'correctly'. Correctness is key here. I would not want to sacrifice the correctness just so I can say my horse can perform canter pirouette on a loose rein if it is a poor canter pirouette. If taking a stronger contact on the reins would help my horse find a better quality canter pirouette, then I would. There is nothing to be gained by letting a horse flounder in mediocrity so you can ride on a loose rein.

I think to argue that a horse being ridden correctly with slack in the reins is evading the bit, is to forget the purpose of contact. The final judgment of a rider's skill stops with the horse and how it responds. At its best, the dialogue between a rider and a horse should appear as a secret.

SOFTNESS

What Is Softness?

Summary: *Softness is a state of emotional well-being that comes from a horse's focus and clarity, and results in minimum resistance.*

Softness is the culmination of focus and clarity. It is the third element that forms the basis of all good horsemanship, and without it, a horse is no more than an obedient slave. A horse cannot be made to be soft because it comes from within a horse being comfortable with going along with a rider's ideas. Softness cannot be imposed on a horse by outside forces.

Many people confuse softness with lightness. They believe that if a horse is responsive to pressure and obeys our direction with very little input from our aids, it must be soft. It is naïve to believe that anytime we don't have to pull hard with the reins or kick hard with our legs, our horse is soft. There is an important difference between softness and lightness. Confusing the two will only lead to a troubled relationship with a horse.

So to be absolutely clear:

- Lightness is a physical response to pressure.
- Softness is an emotional response to pressure.

These are two entirely different things. A horse can be light, but not soft, because it can be highly responsive to pressure and at the same time feel troubled by it and have hard thoughts. It is normal for a horse like this to be so worried by pressure that it does anything it can to avoid it. Often a horse's response to give to pressure is to escape it rather than yield to it. People sacrifice a horse's emotional well-being for the sake of lightness, but a horse can feel light and also be troubled inside.

A soft horse is always relaxed and emotionally comfortable, while still light to the aids. The soft horse is responsive to subtle forms of pressure, yet remains untroubled. In fact, a truly soft horse gets comfort from pressure because pressure offers clarity to how it can find comfort. Therefore, a horse that is light to the aids is not necessarily a soft horse, but a soft horse is always light to the aids.

This might be a good place to also mention a 'soft feel', because many trainers and clinicians discuss soft feel in their teaching. Some people speak about a soft feel in the same breath that they talk about softness as if they were the same thing. They confuse the two concepts.

A soft feel does not require a horse to be in a quiet emotional state, in the same that way softness does. A soft feel comes from lightness, in that the rider only needs to offer a light pressure to evoke a soft feel from a horse. Most times a soft feel is referred to when a rider increases the feel of the reins a small amount in order to induce a horse to offer vertical flexion of the neck. Unless a horse is emotionally calm and there is a flow of softness through the whole length of the horse, and not just from the poll to the wither, then the flexion of the neck represents only lightness and not softness.

Nevertheless, like most things related to horses, softness is not all or nothing. A horse is never absolutely soft and rarely 100 percent resistant. All horses are somewhere in-between most of the time. Our job as trainers is to take the confused horse that nature gave us and spend the rest of our days working towards transforming it into a perfectly soft horse, all the time. We may never achieve 100 percent softness in a horse, but that goal gives us our direction when it comes to working with a horse.

When softness is lacking, look back at your horse's focus and/or your clarity, because the lack of softness originates from an issue with one or both of those elements. It's important to remember that even though a horse's movement comes from its physical side, the quality of the movement comes from the mental and emotional side.

A Quiet Mind

Summary: *A quiet mind is an alert, but relaxed mind. A quiet mind is both achieved through softness and also a necessary component of softness.*

A quiet mind is both what your horse needs in order to be soft, but also what softness gives your horse. So a quiet mind is both the cause of softness and the result of softness. Confusing, isn't it?

A few years ago I was helping a girl whose horse was anxious about being separated from its paddock companion. My student rode her horse to the back gully of her property and I walked alongside. The companion horse, which was left behind, was waiting at the gate in the adjacent paddock.

Everything went well, until towards the end of the lesson, my student's horse became very excited and threatened to bolt when heading back towards the companion horse. My student clearly needed help.

I reached for one rein while I stood next to the horse and the student stayed in the saddle. I used the rein to block the horse's thoughts to leave or push on the rein. I waited and waited until the horse's mind became quiet and was soft in my hand. It had hardly moved its feet, yet it couldn't have made a bigger change in its energy level if it had just run a 100 km race. It was a perfect gentleman the rest of the ride back.

Even though my student had witnessed the entire sequence, she didn't know what I had done to exact a change in her horse. What I did is the basis of everything I try to get across to people about softness. What I did with the horse was block the thoughts I didn't want and waited until it had a quiet mind. I released for the quiet mind.

So what is a quiet mind?

A quiet mind is a restful mind, a settled mind and a mind that is not working on a plan. A quiet mind is not a sleepy mind or a dull mind. It is alert, it is waiting, but it is peaceful and untroubled. People talk about an athlete being "in the zone" and I equate a horse with a quiet mind as being in the zone.

When a horse is bothered, the mind cannot be quiet. An anxious horse has a busy mind, because it is constantly searching for a better way to find comfort and safety. A horse's inside bubbles away and churns over at high speed.

The trick becomes to recognize a horse whose mind is quiet. Many people confuse dull or shut down minds with quiet ones. I think such horses are quiet only on the outside and often have a lot of turmoil inside. Their minds are not quiet, just their feet. You can usually tell this by the lack of responsiveness in such horses.

I think when we talk about the 'happy' horse, we are really talking about a horse that has a quiet mind; the insides are calm. When you see a horse working that has a busy mind, you can be sure it does not feel okay inside. Whether or not a horse has a quiet mind is my personal test of a horse that is comfortable with the training.

I have spent many years trying to tell people about what is a soft horse or what does a horse feel like when it feels okay. It's always been a struggle to put these ideas in ways that have meaning for people. When I really break it down to the essentials, I realize I am just talking about a horse having a quiet mind. The quiet mind leads to softness and you can't have softness without it.

Why Is Softness Important?

Summary: *Softness in a horse culminates in all the elements coming together that make up good horsemanship. Softness is about a horse presenting with a relaxed willingness. Without softness a horse will offer no more than obedience and less than its best performance.*

To have a horse that is soft to work with should be the ultimate goal of any horsemanship. Good horsemanship is the craft of turning the unwilling into the willing. Any other approach to horsemanship is nothing more than bullying a horse into obedience.

Softness forms the basis of everything that is good and of high quality in whatever discipline we choose to ride. Only a horse that is soft can perform at its best, because without softness, a horse is diverting too much energy into mental and physical resistance to be able to do its best work.

In modern competition, I believe there is a disproportionate attention given to rewarding horses with the most extravagant movements. In dressage, we reward the extreme foreleg movement, while ignoring poor hindquarter engagement and false collection. In reining, we reward the fastest spinning horses and ignore the chomping on the bit. In jumping events, the horse with the clear round and the fastest time wins irrespective of how out of control the horse may be. Selective breeding has made all this possible because we can now produce amazingly athletic horses that don't require softness to perform physically demanding movements.

The consequence is that people can now take shortcuts with the training because they no longer require a truly soft horse in order to win an event.

You might ask then, why bother with the time and effort to train a horse to be soft if I can buy a horse that is genetically enhanced to win without it?

I think there are two reasons why softness is important for the majority of people.

The first reason why I believe softness should be important to every horse person is that softness comes from a horse sensing there is no reason to feel bad about their training. Most people have horses because they care about them. A large part of that caring is the desire to make a horse's life as comfortable as possible. A horse that is not soft is in emotional turmoil. A horse that is soft to handle and soft to ride is emotionally comfortable. I believe that is the best reason for striving towards softness.

Secondly, when a horse is soft, it is using its body with straightness and balance. In biomechanical terms, it is working efficiently and correctly to distribute the workload equally through its body. This reduces the risk of physical stress on a horse that can lead to premature soundness problems. Long-term soundness is an issue for every horse and the best insurance is for a horse to be worked with correctness and softness.

The third reason is that not everybody can afford to purchase horses that are so selectively well bred. And if you can afford such a horse, most of them are not easy to ride. When shortcuts are taken with the training, it leaves resistance and anxiety simmering away inside a horse. This means that often times, the horse's idea and the rider's idea are not the same. There is a constant conflict between rider and horse. The reason that gadgets, such as tie-downs or methods such as hyperflexion, have been invented is to physically overcome a horse's resistance that results from taking shortcuts. Taking the time to produce a horse that is soft negates the need for such approaches.

Nearly all sectors of the horse industry in some way talk about the ultimate goal of their discipline as the horse and rider working in harmony and partnership together. This is only possible through softness. It is the degree of softness that gives quality to the movement.

The Road To Softness

Summary: *Softness can only be achieved via thin layers of improvement in focus and clarity. Each small incremental improvement builds on the one before. If problems arise, it is only because the preceding work did not have a high enough standard of softness. Softness can't be achieved by taking giant steps in the training, but requires a thorough coverage of focus and clarity at each step along the way.*

Everything discussed in this book incorporates part of the journey towards softness. Attaining softness in a horse is a process that requires a range of elements coming together to make it work. It's not one thing.

In a nutshell, softness is achieved by the draining away of resistance in a horse. When a horse is focused and clear about working with a human, the ill feelings that imbue resistance are lost and replaced with feelings of comfort and calm that result in softness. When a rider has mastered the elements of focus and clarity in training, then softness is a gift that comes from within the horse.

In the beginning of training, a horse's life is often turned up-side down. At first, this can cause fear and anxiety, resulting in very little softness. A horse can be resistant and unhappy. In extreme cases, they can be belligerent and dangerous. We begin at the beginning by addressing problems with focus. Small changes in being able to keep a horse's thoughts, lead to small changes in being able to direct a horse's thoughts. It's small to begin with, but it's never insignificant. People watching might not have seen any change, but a horse always feels it.

The almost unnoticeable alteration in a horse's focus, followed by almost imperceptible improvements in being able to direct its focus opens the door to a thin shaft of clarity that steals into a horse's understanding of what the human is talking about. When this occurs, the road to softness has begun.

The purpose of years devoted to training is to chip away at problems with a horse's focus and clarity. Layer upon layer of resistance is peeled away. With each layer removed we reveal improvements in a horse's softness. Any time that softness is lost, it's because the degree of focus and clarity was not good enough for the task we asked of our horse at the time.

It's like learning any new task. You can't learn to add or subtract numbers until you learn to count. You can't learn to multiply and divide until you learn to add and subtract. You can't learn algebra until you can add, subtract, multiply and divide. And you can't learn how to perform quadratic equations until you learn algebra. Anytime you have a problem with one of those steps, you need to go back a level and address the problem with what came before.

Building softness into a horse is no different. If we have an issue with our horse lacking softness when leading, we might need to look at the level of focus when we are standing next to it. Or we might need to fix a lack of clarity to our horse's understanding of the feel of the lead rope. When we do that and it leads with more focus and clarity, we might expect it will lead with better softness.

However, what if our horse doesn't lead with improved softness? Perhaps we need to refine the level of focus even more. Or perhaps we need to make the meaning of the feel of the lead rope even clearer than before.

As you can see, all the little changes we might have to make are just variations of refining the focus and clarity in the steps that came before we lost the softness in our horse.

The other factor that needs consideration is the role of consistency in our work. On our journey to instilling softness, we have to be vigilant not to leave a brace in a horse. This is where consistency is so important. Any time we ask a horse to do something, we must to be alert and mindful that the degree of resistance at each step is less than it was before.

How Do You Know When You Have Achieved Softness?

Summary: *As a horse becomes softer, there are improvements in response to pressure, a quiet mind and a decrease in anxiety when a horse's thoughts are interrupted.*

How can a person know when they have achieved softness?

Firstly, as I have said before a horse is never completely soft inside and out. Even in the most highly educated horse there is always a hint of resistance because a horse will always consider its options. This is as it should be.

When considering whether or not your horse is softer, there are two factors to test.

I have already said that softness incorporates lightness to the aids. Therefore, as a horse becomes softer the rider should be aware of the horse responding to less pressure. It does not matter what the source of the pressure is (reins, legs, flag, lead rope, spur, whip etc). As a horse becomes softer, it should require less energy from a rider to achieve a better response from a horse.

The second factor is that as a horse becomes softer, there should be a growing emotional calmness. Again, this is a quiet mind. It is the culmination of focus and clarity growing together in a dominant fashion that produces softness. Softness improves as a result of improvement in the focus and clarity of a horse. The increasing development of focus and clarity nurtures a quiet mind.

However, a quiet mind differs from a dull horse in a very important aspect. When a horse as a quiet mind, not only does it feel relaxed, but it also is not emotionally troubled when we ask for a change of thought. A lot of horses seem to be untroubled until you ask for them to make a change. However, a soft horse is not bothered when you try to replace one thought with another.

As I have said before, the only change worth having is a change of thought. Without a horse changing its thought, there can be no softness. Keeping that in mind, it seems obvious that checking to see if a horse changed its thought is also an appropriate test of whether a horse changed its level of softness.

Therefore, to test if your horse is softer, you should repeat the exercise to confirm if there is less resistance to what you ask, the horse is emotionally quieter yet prepared and the rider's attempt to interrupt the horse's thought does not create any further anxiety.

Balancing Softness

Summary: *It is important that we are vigilant about working towards softness in everything we do with a horse. We should strive to make softness a normal part of our horse's working life. However, in our effort to attain softness, we need to be mindful that improvements are achieved in small steps and not expect too much, too soon, from a horse.*

The idea of having a horse soft all the time is an impossible concept. All the same, we should work toward it in everything we do. This applies to when we pat our horses, halter, trailer load, canter pirouette, sliding stop, pull a log, run barrels, halt, wash their tail. There is no part of our interaction with a horse that we don't want to be soft.

That means that every time we are aware of a resistance or ill feelings in our horse, we have a job to help fix it. We should not be satisfied with just getting a horse to carry out our idea or tolerate our actions. We should endeavour to always improve the softness with which a horse does their job.

Of course, there is a balance between picking on every little thing so a horse feels it can do nothing right, and being vigilant to ensure you reward every try in a horse. This is where the concept of balance comes into building softness. If we pick on a horse too much, or not enough, softness will remain elusive.

The balance between the two forces can be determined by being aware of how much try a horse has in its search for answers. When a horse is struggling to find softness, but is searching hard, then our tolerance of mistakes should be much greater.

However, one-by-one, bit-by-bit, you cross these moments of resistance or ill feelings off your list of problems to fix. It's not a job that has an end. Trying to reach the ultimate in softness is like trying to reach the horizon.

RELATIONSHIP

I have talked extensively about focus, clarity and softness as the basis of all good horsemanship. These are the elements that should be part of everything we do with our horses. I have talked about the goal of good horsemanship as not simply to train a horse to be an obedient slave, but to offer it safety and comfort so that the horse benefits from the relationship as much as the human.

In my view, the ultimate goal of good horsemanship is to have a harmonious relationship with a horse that approaches unity or partnership. Winston Churchill said, "There is nothing better for the inside of a man than the outside of a horse". I think Churchill's quote is not quite accurate, because he infers that the value of a horse is in what it can do for us. I would re-phrase Churchill's quote to suggest that there is nothing better for the inside of a person than the inside of a horse.

Not enough people value the inside of a horse. I think when we do things right in keeping the emotional needs of a horse in the forefront of all our work, we have the potential to form an emotional bond that works both ways, and can come close to what people call a true partnership. Once you have experienced a true partnership with a horse the first time, it is impossible to not want it with every horse you meet.

In this section I want to talk about the relationships that we form with horses.

The Ethics Of Working With Horses

Summary: *We should all examine the ethics of what we do with horses. I believe the ethics of the Middle Ages on using animals no longer applies today, and how we handle and care for horses (and other animals) should be decided by the highest concern for the physical and emotional welfare of horses.*

Before discussing about our relationship with horses, I want to briefly talk about the ethics of working with horses, and the responsibilities that arise from them.

From time to time I am asked, that given my views on horses and training, why do I ride horses at all? Apparently, if I really cared about a horse's welfare and their comfort, I should just let them roam freely and never ride or train them.

The first time I was asked this, my immediate reaction was that it was a silly question. But years later, I can see that it is a question all horse people should ask themselves, so they are clear in their own mind regarding the type of relationship they are working towards with a horse.

Surprisingly, there is still some argument in the horse world whether horses have emotions at all. I think this dates back to the 13th century, when philosophers such as Thomas Aquinas proclaimed animals were not worthy of consideration because it was assumed they could not reason as humans. This makes sense for those times because most philosophers were also theologians and their belief system put humans as God's children and animals were a gift from God for the benefit of humans.

Thankfully, only a handful of people still hold those views.

However, there is still considerable stigma in anthropomorphizing, or assigning human-like qualities (like emotions) to animals. These days, many people believe that to anthropomorphize animals is wrong.

Personally, I believe anthropomorphism is a positive thing on the whole and is completely justified. The problem comes from people taking anthropomorphism too far. For example, clearly horses have the neural network capable of experiencing emotions, so it is perfectly reasonable to suggest they can experience suffering.

Even so, horses don't have the brain mechanisms to plot and scheme, so it is not reasonable to assume that horses can try to trick us or plot against us. Yet, people want to make the issue of anthropomorphism black and white, i.e. either horses share human-like qualities or they don't. The reality is that they share some, but not all.

Anybody who has spent time with horses will know that they can exhibit fear, joy, nervousness, relaxation, curiosity and many other emotions. They can make decisions between two or more choices, which I consider a form of reasoning or problem solving. So it is not unreasonable to assign human-like qualities to a horse, if it helps people have a better understanding of how they operate.

Scientists are only catching up to what horse people have known for centuries with regard to the emotional nature of horses and all species with a complex central nervous system. It's been shown that there are common centres of the brain across all vertebrates that relate to the emotional capacity of an animal. In particular the amygdala is similar in humans, horses, birds, fish, and amphibians. Studies have shown that if the thinking part of the brain is destroyed, but the amygdala is left intact, rats still show emotionally-driven behaviour. I don't think it is too much of a stretch to consider that horses would exhibit similar responses.

To me, this makes perfect sense when you consider that evolution works by small modifications to create a new species. Most species of vertebrates have more DNA in common, than different. So it is a much more rational argument to consider that humans differ from horses as a matter of degree, rather than as two species radically and completely different.

The bottom line is that all species with a complex brain (including horses) have an emotional nature that is hardwired into them. As we know, horses are not automatons, but animals with strong emotional needs that largely determine how they behave in the world. If we deny the emotional nature of a horse as the primary motivator for behaviour and response to training, then we deny the true nature of the animal. Emotions drive everything.

When I have talked about the link between a horse's emotions and thoughts in the past, I have been asked, "How can you know what a horse is thinking and feeling?"

The inference is that I can't possibly know what a horse is thinking and feeling because horses don't sit down with us over a cup of tea and tell us their problems. However, they do tell us. They are always telling us. In fact, they hardly ever shut up!

People make the mistake of confusing their inability to listen to a horse, as the horse's inability to talk to us. It is the arrogance of human nature for us to believe that because we don't understand something, it does not exist.

The 18th century German philosopher, Arthur Schopenhauer believed that suffering should determine the ethics of all our decisions in life, and in this regard, we should empathize with the suffering of animals.

If you agree with Schopenhauer, then the ethics of horse training is an easy choice. The emotional well-being of the horse should be the most important determinant in the methods of training we choose. Other factors, such as obedience and competitive success, should play minor roles in the choice of training approaches we adopt.

Having given you the entire preamble about ethics, how do I justify training horses instead of letting them roam untouched in my paddocks?

In my mind, the justification lies in the choices I make. I choose not to do things with horses that I believe are not to their benefit. For example, I keep my horses in as natural environment as possible. I choose methods and equipment that I have a thorough understanding of how and why to use. I work towards a better relationship in everything I do with a horse, and strive to never stop being the student.

It's not for me to preach to others about the ethics of training horses. Each person has his or her own ethics and values. Nevertheless, I urge everybody to have at the forefront of their minds when working with a horse, that everything they do should be judged foremost in terms of the emotional well-being of each and every horse.

"The greatness of a nation and its moral progress can be judged by the way its animals are treated" – Mahatma Ghandi

Abuse Of Horses

Summary: *When we talk about a good relationship with a horse, we are automatically talking about a non-abusive relationship. However, not many people agree on what constitutes abuse. I believe that everything we do with a horse needs to be weighed in terms of the benefits it offers to a horse. In that way, we reduce the risk of steering our relationship down the wrong path.*

In any discussion on ethics, we should consider the topic of abuse.

It's not hard to get people to agree that abuse is both wrong and damaging to a good relationship. However, it is hard to get everyone to agree on a definition of abuse.

It is imperative that we are all absolutely certain about our personal definition of what is abuse, because this defines our decisions about the methods and practices we find acceptable or not acceptable when we work with horses.

For me, abuse is anything we inflict on a horse that does not benefit a horse.

By my definition, I guess you could make a list of abuses that would fill a large book. Anything from beating a horse with a cricket bat to rugging on a warm day can constitute abuse. It is never black and white, and there are an infinite number of degrees of abuse.

Is it just as cruel to ride in an ill-fitting saddle, as it is to keep a horse in a paddock by itself? Who knows? Is it just as bad to hobble a horse to make it stand still for saddling, as it is to beat a horse for not standing still? Who decides? Is it just as abusive to dock a horse's tail for the sake of beauty, as it is to not trim his feet regularly? Who knows? In my opinion, all these things are an abuse because they are of no benefit to the horse, either in the medium or long-term.

I believe abuse can take a much broader meaning than just not looking after the physical needs of a horse.

Harry Whitney has described a lack of clarity as a form of horse abuse. While I agree with this completely, I think the concept can be applied more widely to anything humans do that leaves a horse emotionally unsettled. We can cater to all of our horses' physical needs of food, shelter, living in a natural environment, health care etc., yet we abuse our horses through training that is unclear and emotionally disturbing. I can't stress enough that in my view, a training philosophy that does not lead to a quiet mind is just as abusive as starving a horse.

I'm not trying to force my definition or values regarding abuse on anybody. This is not an area where right and wrong are written in stone, but I am trying to provide something for people to think about. I'm sure we all agree that starving a horse is cruel, but what about a slightly less obvious example like using a drop noseband to keep a horse's mouth shut? Is that cruel? What advantage does a noseband have for the horse? In what way does a noseband help the horse feel better? These are the sorts of questions that challenge us to provide a definition of abuse that satisfies each of us.

What Is A Partnership?

Summary: *The term partnership is too easily bandied about as meaning that a horse performs well and doesn't try to kill its owner. However, much more is involved. Even if a person is never likely to have a true partnership with a horse, we should still try, every day. It also means we love and respect a horse for the amazing creature it is.*

In my opinion, the ultimate goal of working with a horse is to have a fulfilling partnership that works both ways. It's the final outcome of having focus, clarity and softness. It is the fruit that bears when the training goes well. It doesn't matter what interest or pursuit you follow in your training, the best it can be is when you have a good partnership with a horse.

I have heard it said many times by people about what a good partnership they have with their horse. In my experience, that usually means that their horse doesn't play up very much, and they do fairly well in competition. I think many people mistake partnership with obedience and submission. They believe a good partnership exists when a horse does what it is told without much fuss. However, I don't think that is the same thing as having a true partnership.

In my opinion, a true partnership is a relationship you have where both parties choose to be in it. In a partnership there is no submission, coercion or slavish obedience. In a partnership, both parties profit from the relationship, which becomes the reason they have for choosing to be in the partnership.

When we talk about a partnership with our horses, it's easy to see what we get out of it, but what do our horses get from it? Is it enough to call it a partnership because we provide our horse with food and veterinary care? Is that enough incentive for our horses to choose to be in a partnership with us?

I believe that doesn't count. Caring for the physical needs of a horse is a minimum responsibility of just being an owner, not a partner. Horses are not concerned with an expensive saddle or having its feet trimmed. Apart from having a full belly, a horse's primary concern is for their psychological and emotional needs, such as being maintained in a herd and not having their safety jeopardized. If we can't fulfill those needs, we can't attain a good partnership with a horse, in spite of the expensive feed, saddle, lessons and rugs.

So what else does a horse need in order to choose to hang out with us?

I believe a horse needs to feel good in our company and when working with us. We have to offer a horse comfort and relaxation and the least amount of stress possible. We have to offer a horse a good place to be, so that it would choose to be with us of its own free will. Until we can offer a horse those things, I don't think we can truly say we have a partnership with our horse.

Without those things in place I believe the best relationship we can expect is employer and employee. That's not necessarily a bad thing, and in fact it is probably better than a lot of people have with their horse, but it is far from the goal that many of us wish we had of being in partnership with our horse.

I believe than any training that involves the use of pressure that takes away a horse's choices, is going in the wrong direction of ever obtaining a partnership. Training that uses pressure to force a horse to do something is going to get in the way of a partnership. The use of gadgets, pain and fear are just creating obedience and submission.

Partnerships between people and horses are extremely rare, because even with the best intentions, it is difficult to convince a horse to give something more than just its obedience.

My Experiences Of Partnership

Summary: *We all talk about our relationship with our horses and like to think of it as a positive relationship for both parties, but I believe there is a deepness to some relationships that can only be attained when the horse and the human become co-dependent. In a relationship like this, some things are just understood between the two that are not taught or trained. I don't know how it develops or what it is, but I do believe it is real, even if it is rare.*

I am convinced that when a partnership is formed, a horse is capable of offering a try that is beyond the narrow confines that training teaches. Horses are so much more capable of giving than we are capable of teaching. I want to describe some examples from my own experiences of what I believe can happen as the result of a good partnership between a horse and rider.

A while back I came across some old diaries. They were from my horse trekking days through the eastern states of Australia. Whenever I did a long distance ride I kept a record of day-to-day events. It was interesting to go through the pages and have the memories flood back. Some things I had forgotten about, some things I wish I had forgotten about, but most were great memories of younger days and great adventures.

I have done a lot of trekking on horseback in past years, with trips spanning from three weeks to eight months. All of them were solo treks, traversing up and down the eastern parts of Australia using no more than two horses – a riding horse and a pack horse.

I hadn't talked very much to my wife Michèle, about my long distance travels on horseback, but one day she asked me what did I learn about horses after living with them every day? I really had to think about it.

At first, I thought about all the survival techniques I had learned like catching birds, rabbits and fish with my hands, building bridges out of tree bark, lighting fires in the rain, etc. Yet, nothing really jumped out at me about what I had learned about horses that only came from my long distance travelling. However, since then I've had time to reflect.

When you live with horses every minute of every day for week after week and month after month, you become co-dependent on each other. It's a very different relationship than the one where you ride a horse every day for a job, then put it back in the paddock until the next day. It's a strange thing to explain, but you become so dependent on each other that nothing is more important than your horses.

I think I can best explain it with some of true-life adventures.

I have already mentioned in the Clarity section about the incident where I was camped in the western districts of Victoria, Australia and I had an accident with the campfire where I slightly burned my eyes and was unable to see for several days. It was my horse, China, who was able to lead me to the creek each day to wash out my eyes. I would hold onto his tail and follow as he negotiated fallen logs and thick lantana bush to take me to the water. China would wait patiently while I washed my eyes and body, and filled water containers. Sometimes he would have a drink and sometimes not. Either way, he stood quietly until I indicated it was time to lead me back to camp. I had never taught China to lead from the tail. Yet, somehow he understood.

There was another time camped in the gorge country of northern New South Wales. I knew there were wild horses (brumbies) in the area, so I tied my horses to a hi-line and hobbled them in case the brumbies encroached on the camp to take Luke and China during the night.

In the very early morning, I heard brumbies trotting towards the camp. The noise from the hobble chains told me that my horses were very agitated. There was a sudden ruckus of horses crashing through the bush and into the camp. By the time I was out of bed and found my flashlight, the tail end of the five or six brumbies were all that I could see. I looked toward the trees where I left Luke and China tied, but there was nothing there to see but broken ropes. Thinking they had gone with the brumbies I turned towards a noise coming from behind me. My horses were hobbling towards the camp with the remainder of the ropes dangling from their halters. Even though they were hobbled I knew they could have left with the wild horses if they wished. Hobbles don't impede a horse from moving; they just make sure they tire quicker. I don't know why they chose to stay close to camp, but I was so thankful they did.

On another occasion when I was camping in the mountains, a couple of hikers wandered into my camp late at night. One of their members, back at their own camp, was ill. The group sent two people ahead to find a farm and a car. When they saw the glow of my campfire they thought I must be a camper with a car. You can imagine how disappointed they were that I only had horses. Anyway, I agreed to go back to their camp with my two horses and then take their sick friend to a town about thirty kilometers away, over the other side of the mountain.

After I loaded the fellow onto my horse, Luke, we headed out over the mountain in the pitch black of night. Luke followed me on China and we bashed our way through the thick bush. There were no tracks and it was impossible to see more than a few feet in front of us. I had to constantly turn on my flashlight to be sure we were not about to step off a cliff.

My passenger was not a rider, and was obviously too ill to hold on. He fell off Luke several times. The only way I knew he had fallen was because I could no longer hear Luke behind me. Luke halted the instant he sensed his passenger lose balance and fall. Instead of continuing to keep up with China and I, Luke stopped and waited until I backtracked and helped the patient back into the saddle. Luke did this several times through the night until we eventually found a farm where the owner was able to drive the ill man to a local hospital.

I don't know how Luke knew he was to stop and wait. Normally, Luke's first priority was to keep up with China and I, but somehow he knew he had a different job of waiting for his passenger to be hoisted back into the saddle. Just like I don't know how China and Luke knew to stay near the camp and not run with the brumbies. Or how China understood his job was to lead a blind man to water. They just knew.

The bonding and fellowship that can develop between a person and a horse can be much stronger than most of us get a chance to discover. At its best, a partnership with a horse brings out something inside a horse where it fills in the gaps between the training. A horse is able to offer far more than any training teaches. I believe the principles of good horsemanship are a first step to building that kind of relationship.

But Why Would He?

Summary: *Many of the limitations we experience in our training of horses stem from our low expectations of how it should be. Often times, good enough is just that, and we allow our relationship to fall short of what is possible. When we try to prevent a horse from acting out, instead of addressing the cause of bad behaviour, we become the limiting factor in the relationship.*

A lot of people appear to have low expectations of their horses. They seem to accept bad and unpredictable behaviour from their horse as normal and part of being a horse.

Many years ago a woman sent her horse to me for some riding education. At our first meeting she presented me with a long list of things her horse did. The list did not itemise the things she wanted addressed in the training, they were just to let me know what to expect from her horse. The list included pawing when tied up, pulling away when being hosed, kicking when you try to pick up a back leg, wouldn't stand still to be mounted, and aggression at feeding time. She happily lived with the things on the list and saw no reason why they needed fixing.

The woman was not aware that the items on her list were telling her something important about the quality of relationship she had with her horse. If her horse felt okay and her relationship was good, her list would be blank.

A while ago I got into a conversation with a person who was saying that she teaches her horses to never turn their bum towards her. I asked her why and she said because he can't kick at her if he can't have his rear end facing her.

I said that it didn't bother me if my horse's bum was facing me. She fired back, "But what if he tries to kick you?"

"But why would he?" I responded.

"But what if he did?" she asked.

"But why would he?"

"But what if he did?"

Clearly, she was not getting the answer she wanted.

I may have given her an unsatisfactory answer, but it was a legitimate answer. I was trying to get the woman to ask herself about her own horse, "Why would he?"

At a clinic awhile back, a rider was about to mount her horse. Before putting her foot in the stirrup she took a hold of the reins and tightened them up so the bit was pulling in her horse's mouth. I asked her why she shortened the reins, and she said, "So he won't walk away while I get on."

I said, "But why would he?"

"But he might, and I need to be stop him before he does it."

"But why would he?"

I asked her to let the reins hang loose and the horse stood quietly while she mounted.

If people asked themselves, why would he? They might get an insight into how things are between them and their horse.

When it comes to my own horses, I have not taught them to stand still when I mount, they just do. I have not put any time into training them to tie up or load onto a float, they just do. Likewise, I do not get concerned if my horse's rear end is facing me. Kicking at me doesn't even cross their minds or mine.

Horses do things for a reason. They walk away for a reason when a person mounts. They pull back for a reason when tied up. They turn their rear to kick at things for a reason. All these things are based on what a horse believes to be good and solid reasons. A horse doesn't kick at a person just because that person is in the firing line. And it doesn't walk away when a person puts their foot in the stirrup just because the person has a loose rein.

If the horse feels okay about being mounted or feels safe when a person is behind them, they have no reason to act defensively when these things happen. It comes back to how thoroughly we get our horses feeling okay for what is about to happen. Preparation is the key.

If you have a horse that kicks when a person is behind them, then prepare the horse before it happens. Help it feel there is no need to kick at the person. Don't punish the horse for turning its rear end towards you. That goes back to what I believe about not punishing a horse for having the feelings it has. It's not good horsemanship and it's not good relationship-building. Instead, help replace the poor feelings with good ones and things will be a lot safer.

Likewise, if a horse walks away before the rider is seated in the saddle, then fix the feelings that make the horse want to leave. For instance, getting on a horse that is squirming and fidgeting even before you try to mount is ensuring trouble when you put a foot in the stirrup and setting your horse up for failure and criticism. Instead, do some ground work first that has the horse feeling soft and mellow. When it feels okay inside, it won't be in a hurry to walk away when you mount.

It doesn't matter what the situation may be. It might be riding along the road and keeping a tight rein in case the horse tried rushing home or perhaps using a twitch in case the horse flung its head when you tried to worm paste it. In everything we train, it is important to be mindful of the horse's thoughts and feelings as the root cause of every issue.

The long-term success of our relationship with a horse comes from changing the feelings that cause the horse trouble. It doesn't come from creating enough resistance to block a behaviour, or troubling a horse enough for doing the wrong thing. It comes from altering the turmoil that causes the problem. It is amazing how many things just get better because the horse feels better without having to address each individual problem.

The Myth Of Gentle Horsemanship

Summary: *The notion of 'gentle horsemanship' has nothing to do with good horsemanship. If a person is effective at doing as little as possible, but as much as necessary to achieve a change of thought in a horse, then there is no difference in the level of gentleness between methods of training a horse. This is sometimes a hard concept for people to accept because it seems a no-brainer that using a whip is more cruel than using a feather. The purpose of clarity is to be as effective in getting a change of thought as possible, which in turn, is as gentle an approach to training as there can be.*

This might be a good time to talk about the concept of 'gentle horsemanship'. You don't have to look hard to find advertisements where trainers are promoting themselves as only using gentle or kind methods in their horsemanship. On the internet, people ask for recommendations for trainers who only use gentle methods. People are attracted to the idea of using methods that are kind to their horse, because they believe that it will lead to a good relationship with their horse.

However, I think the idea of 'gentle horsemanship' is a misnomer. I caution people about getting caught up in the emotions of wanting to only use gentle methods with their horse. I'll try to explain why I believe terms like gentle and kind are more about us than it is about our horses.

The reason why I believe there is no such thing as gentle methods is simple. For a horse to be motivated to change its idea, carrying out that idea needs to become less comfortable than the idea we want it to try. A horse makes choices based on what it perceives is in its best interest. In order to encourage a horse to change, we need to make the thing it wants to do less comfortable.

This inevitably places a stress on a horse because discomfort is always associated with some degree of stress.

Each horse has a threshold of pressure that, in its eyes, makes the thing it wants to do not worth doing anymore. It is the minimum amount of pressure and stress that it needs to experience in order to decide to change its thought.

This is different for each horse because horses have different sensitivity to pressure. To get the same degree of change in a sensitive horse may take a fraction of the pressure it does for an unflappable horse. Within each horse, the bare minimum, or threshold amount of pressure needed to change a horse's thought creates the same level of anxiety. The level of anxiety we introduce in order to motivate a horse to change, is always the same across all horses.

What I am trying to say is that in order to change a thought, a sensitive horse feels just as stressed by a small amount of pressure as a stoic horse feels with a lot of pressure. Both horses experience the same degree of anxiety even though different amounts of pressure were used.

Therefore, the approach used on one horse was no kinder or crueler than the one used on the other horse. The approaches had the same degree of gentleness (from a horse's point of view), irrespective of how firmly the method was applied.

It's not the amount of pressure or energy you apply during training that determines the level of kindness or cruelty. Rather, it's the horse's perception. If we use just enough pressure to motivate a horse to search for a new answer, we are using the gentlest amount of pressure possible, while still being effective. It doesn't matter if one person applies one approach to training and another uses a completely different approach. If they are being effective in getting a change of thought and doing the least amount as possible, both approaches are identical in their level of gentleness.

Prey/Predator Relationships In Training

Summary: *I don't think there is much credibility in the prey/predator model to base the training of horses upon. It is inaccurate, and skews the way we look at our relationship with horses in a way that hinders how close a relationship we can achieve. Furthermore, it adds nothing to our understanding of horses that is useful in the training process.*

You have probably heard people talking about the human/horse relationship being based on the predator/prey relationship. This idea has been polluting the thinking of horse people, and particularly natural horsemanship, for decades. In my opinion, it has little merit in affecting how we relate to our horses.

Some horse people have taken a small bit of scientific information about prey versus predator behaviour and blown it into a whole philosophical approach to training horses that is largely without justification. It comes from trying to make a rational argument out of a few oversimplified concepts.

The theory goes: Horses graze and humans hunt. Horses have a natural fear of animals that hunt and eat meat. Therefore, horses are innately afraid of humans.

However, for this bit of deduction to hold true a horse must be able to recognize a human is a predator that will eat them. So how does a horse identify a predator?

I believe horses recognize predation, not predators. That is, they don't recognize a species as a predator. All the same, they do recognize a behaviour that is predatory. The body language of an animal that is hunting is what sets off alarm bells in horses.

For example, it is well known that zebras do not fear lions that are wandering around the herd. They even tolerate them calmly walking into a herd. However, they do fear a lion when it is stalking a zebra. It is a lion assuming the hunting posture that alerts a zebra, not the fact that a predatory species is in the vicinity. Horses don't categorize the species as friend or foe. Rather, they judge the behaviour of another species as friendly or threatening.

It is true that horses, with little or no experience of humans, are often fearful of people. Even so, they are fearful of narrow spaces too. That does not mean they perceive the narrow space as a predator. Horses are fearful of the unknown. Nonetheless, I don't believe they view every unknown as a predator.

The prey/predator model does not contribute anything useful to our understanding of horse behaviour or horse training. The only thing it tells us is that horses do not like it when we act like we want to kill them. Yet, we already know not to act aggressively towards a horse, dog, bird, gorilla or a grizzly bear, if we want to get along with it.

Behaving aggressively is not the same as behaving as a predator. All species can act aggressively, including horses, squid, bees and millipedes. However, not all species are predators. Predation is a hunting strategy, while aggression is a comfort and safety-seeking strategy. I believe people who talk about the prey/predator relationship are really teaching not to act aggressively or threateningly towards a horse. This is different than behaving like a predator, even though they use the prey/predator analogy to make their point.

I believe people have taken the prey/predator principle out of context.

We know that when a lion stalks a zebra it stares at it with both eyes. Therefore, many people avoid looking directly at a horse for fear of behaving like a predatory lion.

Other people will not stand squarely to a horse, but instead angle their shoulders when facing a horse, so as not to appear confrontational. I've had students come to clinics who will actually turn away from their horse when asking it to walk up to them. I think these ideas are premised on the notion that only a predator would stand square, and therefore that type of behaviour will worry a horse.

I have discovered that these ideas have no real merit when developing a relationship with horses. My dogs will approach a horse squarely and will look at it with both eyes, yet I see no concern about that in the horses. In fact, I have known a horse or two to chase a dog it didn't know out of the paddock. Who is the predator in that case?

I truly believe it is a false premise to think that humans are the natural enemy of the horse.

People Did Not Invent Horse Training

Summary: *Skill as a horse trainer is limited by our ability to understand the work from the horse's perspective and to adapt to the individual needs of each horse. Rules are based on the experience of other people working with other horses, and not on ourselves working with the horse in front of us. If we are going to achieve the ultimate goal of having a true partnership with a horse, we need to thoroughly appreciate this fact.*

To state the obvious, humans did not invent riding and training of horses. Those things were discovered. All the elements that make riding and training possible were already in place before a human ever sat astride the first horse to be ridden. The only thing people did was to discover those elements. They did not create them.

We invented bridles and saddles and round yards, but we did not invent horse training and how best to ride. We discovered it.

I want to make that point because it seems that nowadays many people believe that the rules we have created around how to ride and how to train are golden rules beyond question. The rules are designed to tell us how to ride and train correctly.

However, they are rules made by people out of their experience with horses. Yet horses did not make the rules.

It's not for us to tell a horse how it should respond to anything we do. It's our job to discover how to get the best we can from each horse. When we are training towards a good relationship, we are on a path of discovery that our horse already knows.

For instance, the Fédération Equestre Internationale (FEI) rules state that a horse must be ridden with a noseband in dressage competitions. Since dressage is judged on the performance of the horse, why should a horse that does not need a noseband to give its best performance be required to wear one? The noseband rule is not a horse rule. It's not enough reason to believe that because somebody wrote it in a rulebook it must be it right.

People think that because riding and training are human pursuits, humans make the rules. Certainly, centuries of experience have allowed us to formulate guidelines for riding and training horses. Nonetheless, they are only guidelines and not rules. Horses are all going to be different from each other, but one thing they have in common is they have no innate understanding of human rules.

I understand that if you are going to get serious about competition, you have to be serious about the rules of the governing bodies. It's their sandpit and if you want to play in it, you have to follow their rules. Nevertheless, that is different to saying that their rules are the correct rules. If you want to follow the correct rules, discover your horse's rules, not your friend's horse or your instructor's or your other horse's rules. Don't tell your horse what the rules are. It will tell you, if you are humble enough to listen.

Rules change, fashions change. Rules don't deserve to be strictly followed until they have proved themselves to be the best practice for your horse, and the relationship you want.

Every Relationship Has Its Limits

Summary: *All relationships have their limits. There is a line that if crossed, will damage any relationship. A good relationship with our horses is not measured by how much they hang around us when we sit under a tree in their paddock. It is measured by how they feel when they are asked to commit to doing something. It's when you ask a horse to do something they would not normally choose to do themselves, that you can tell how good is your relationship is with your horse. A friend once told me, "A friend will help you move. A good friend will help you move a body".*

I believe every relationship has it limits. There is a line that if crossed, will lead to turmoil. So when somebody says they have a great relationship with their horse, do they know where that line is?

Often times at a clinic, horses will be highly stressed the first day and not behave as well as their owners expect. People tell me their horse usually does much better at home. They see the behaviour their horse exhibits at the clinic as an aberration and not something to be concerned about because their horse isn't normally like that a home.

In reality, the horse you have at home is not really the horse you have. The way your horse behaves at strange places is the animal you really have. By taking it to a clinic and observing a different behaviour, you have discovered one of the limitations of how strong or weak your relationship really is.

When we are working our horses at home and the sun is shining and the birds are singing, we are often lulled into believing we are doing a great job. Our horse does everything we want with minimal resistance. It seems focused and relaxed. So often this is not the result of us, but of the confidence a horse has in being in a familiar and comfortable environment. A horse can become reliant on a familiar environment to keep it safe and relaxed.

It is inevitable that a day will come when the environment changes. We might have to go somewhere unfamiliar with our horse. It could be a show, or a vet clinic, or a different arena, or a trail ride at a friend's property. It could be riding in a group or by yourself. It could be to a horsemanship clinic or it could be at home on a stormy day. It could be anything that tests the boundaries of your horse's comfort zone.

It's important to know where those boundaries are so you can work to extend them. By stretching the comfort limits of your horse, you build a stronger and more consistent relationship. Your horse will become less reliant on getting used to the environment to feel safe, and more dependent on your leadership and guidance to keep it out of trouble.

You never want to push a horse over the limit of what it can handle, but taking a horse closer towards the edge and bringing it back is highly recommended. Don't leave a horse close to the edge. Make sure you help it find its way back to an emotionally safe spot.

So when you take a horse somewhere and it behaves unlike its normal self, don't think it is an aberration. What the horse is showing you is real, and an indicator of the limits of your relationship. The horse is showing you where you need to be working more on focus, clarity and softness.

There is no great trick to having a contented horse if you never put it under pressure. I have seen people who don't put pressure on a horse and are so happy that their horse is cuddly and smoochy. However, when the day comes that an owner needs to put pressure on a horse, that all changes. Suddenly the horse becomes worried, frightened and sometimes dangerous.

For me, having a good relationship with a horse is not all about a horse being happy to see me or hang out with me. That's part of it, but that alone is not very helpful. A good relationship with a horse stems from being able to direct a change of thought without causing worry to a horse.

If I can't ask for a change of thought without causing anxiety and bad feelings, then there is much more work to do. It doesn't matter how much your horse likes being around you when peace and tranquility reign over the world if those feelings dissipate when you start trying to direct its thoughts.

It's Never Personal: Punishment Offers No Clarity

Summary: *When a horse makes a choice we don't like, it is easy to see this as a challenge to us, as if the horse has a personal vendetta against us. This is not the case. When we assess a horse's misbehaviour as being personal, we are prone to replying with anger and punishment, which is never a positive learning experience for a horse.*

When I was younger I worked at a riding school. As a teenager I loved to jump horses and was fortunate to be offered rides on some good horses. However, I was a moody teenager and prone to anger when a horse refused to do what it was told. I believed that disobedience was not to be tolerated in a horse. Nothing made my blood boil quicker than if a horse knew how to do something I asked, but it refused.

The fellow who owned the riding school was also my mentor and jumping coach. He recognized that I was quick to anger when a horse made a mistake or challenged my authority.

One day the boss said to me that I took the horse's response too personally.

"It's not about you. When he refuses in front of a jump, he isn't doing it to you or to teach you a lesson. It's never personal with a horse. He is just being a horse and you are just being a teenager, but only one of you has a temper problem."

This made a huge impact on me. It never occurred to me that a horse's bad behaviour was not personal. It always felt personal. I thought about it a lot and each time I felt my temper flare, I would try to remember what the boss had said. In time I learned to stop getting angry at horses.

The reason why I think this is such an important lesson is because if we don't substitute anger with compassion, and blame with understanding, we are not open to learning. If we see mistakes as the horse's fault, how can we change what needs changing in ourselves? My anger was a hindrance to me becoming a better horse person, and until somebody pulled me up and pointed out how ignorant I was, nothing was going to get better.

Even more serious is that when we take a horse's resistance as personal, we are prone to punishing it. Punishment is never okay. Punishment is only a way for a person to let off steam and has no learning benefit for the horse. There are no lessons for a horse to learn in his punishment except to say that humans can't be trusted. Punishment is directionless, and only confuses a horse. There is no clarity to be gained from punishing a horse for any transgression. I can't think of any exception to that rule.

Nowadays it seems the truth of this lesson is so obvious I fail to understand how everybody doesn't know it. Unfortunately, when I travel around doing clinics, I sometimes see my younger self in some of the people I meet.

Petting A Horse

Summary: *The purpose of petting a horse should be to touch it in a way that feels good to the horse. In this way, a horse can learn to feel comfortable to be around the human without the need to yield to pressure. Petting in the right way can help build a connection that is interwoven into getting along with a horse. However, when done without feeling, petting has no meaning to a* *horse. At best, it can give a horse a break from being asked to do something. At worst, it becomes something that annoys a horse.*

Petting is something we do the first time we are close to a horse in our life, and every time from then on. It seems almost instinctive to pet a horse several times whenever we encounter one. In fact, most people have trouble resisting touching a horse. We seem to believe that petting a horse is automatically positive for establishing a good relationship.

Yet, despite how frequently we rub, stroke or pat our horses, how often have any of us questioned the why, the how, and the what for, of petting our horse? Why do we do it and what does it mean to the horse? It may seem obvious that petting your horse is the right and proper thing to do. It certainly seems that way to me, but most people never question or think about the serious side of petting a horse.

For most of us, I think petting our horses is a form of greeting when we first approach them. When we put them away after a ride we like to pet them as a farewell gesture. Then during a work session many of us pet our horses as a way of saying "good boy" and letting them know we are pleased with their work. However, does any of this really make sense to a horse? Do we just touch our horses to make us feel good, or does it have real meaning to the horse? Even if we teach a horse our meaning of our touches, does it, or should it care that we are saying 'hello', 'good bye' and 'well done'?

Many years ago I attended a Harry Whitney clinic in the USA. It was the first morning of a five-day clinic and people are sometimes quiet and shy on the first day. Harry often asked me to get some horse conversation going around the table at those times in order to break the ice among people who really didn't know each other. I would often do this by asking people something that might get them thinking about horses.

On this particular morning I decided to ask about petting a horse.

At Harry's prompting I asked, "Why do we pet our horses? What's so important about it? We mostly take it for granted that we should pet our horses, but why and what do horses get out of it?"

Some of the people asked me to explain what I meant, so I did. Then people started getting involved in the discussion.

Somebody said, "Well, I know my horse likes it when I pet him, so I use it as a reward when he is doing the right thing."

Someone else said, "My horse gets so itchy that I like to scratch him to make him feel good."

There were a few more similar responses. Then one woman said, "I know that petting my horse gives me confidence and helps me relax. It's something I can do that won't bother my horse when I am riding and feeling nervous." This led to somebody else suggesting that petting their horse helped calm the horse, as well as themselves.

The conversation continued for some time with both Harry and I sitting back and listening while everybody exchanged views. After a while there was a lull in the conversation and then somebody asked Harry what he thought. Harry didn't give away too much and said he'd like to hear what I believed.

"Well, I'm not too sure what I believe about petting. I do think a lot of how we pet our horses is more about how we feel rather than how we want our horse to feel," I said.

"You know the sort of thing where you see a rider come cantering out of the winner's ring with ribbons adorning their horse and there they are slapping the horse's neck as if they were beating the dust out of an old blanket? That can't feel too good to the horse, yet people do it because it makes them feel good.

"I do believe there is a way to petting your horse that can have a lot of meaning to him. I think if done in a way that really feels good to the horse, you can make contact with something that is deep inside both of you. It's a connection that can go some way to building the trust and bond that we all talk about trying to achieve. I don't know for sure that it is real, but I feel it is."

Harry responded, "I think petting your horse is no different from anything else you do with a horse. If it's going to have a good meaning to the horse, there needs to be a quality of petting that helps establish the connection you want with your horse. You can't fake that quality; you can't hide your true feelings behind the way you pet a horse. He feels the intent and emotion behind your touch."

The conversation when on for a little longer before Harry broke it up with a suggestion that we stop talking and start riding. Everybody headed out to the stalls to gather their horses.

One of the horses brought to the clinic was a Mustang mare. The owner had a few problems with the mare, but the first one she mentioned was that the horse seemed to not like men. She explained that anytime her husband tried to handle the horse the mare would get very nervous and difficult to handle. Harry asked me to ride the horse for the first day of the clinic.

The mare was fairly nervous about me at the start, but she was such a sweet thing that she settled after a few minutes. On the third day of the clinic Harry suggested that the three other men in the clinic handle and ride the little mustang mare in an effort to help her get better with men in her life. The owner seemed fine with the idea.

What the male volunteers didn't know was that Harry had spoken to all the women at the clinic beforehand about what was going to happen.

The three men took their turn ground working and riding the mare. There was a middle-aged cowboy, a much younger man and a mechanic. After this exercise was completed, Harry suggested we all go for lunch. During the meal Harry announced to the men that they had been set up. He had schemed with the women that they should watch each of the men handle the Mustang, and pay particular attention to how they petted the horse. There was a round table conversation where Harry asked each of the women about what they had observed.

The first thing that was interesting was that almost all the women had the same observations. They concluded that the first rider was a little nervous and appeared tentative when he petted the horse. The result was that the horse appeared nervous and unsure.

The second fellow was quiet, but confident around the horse. When he rubbed the horse on the brow, the horse seemed to melt into his hand. They described it as if he was comforting a child after it had a bad dream. All the women felt they could see he made a connection within the horse.

The final male presented himself to the horse as being sure and confident, but at the same time when he petted the horse it seemed to mean nothing to the horse. He rubbed the horse on the brow, but was firm and rough. The women concluded that the horse didn't appear to like this at all.

Long after the clinic was over I kept thinking about petting a horse and what it means. I no longer tell people to pet their horse. Instead, I suggest they "love on" their horse or they "rub their horse with their heart". What I mean by this is that they should not just pat it mindlessly, or rub it like a burned pot to be scoured. Instead, they should try to make contact in a way that really matters to them and their horse.

I don't know for certain what exactly stroking a horse with your heart does for the horse, but I am pretty sure that there is a way of patting or rubbing a horse that makes a big difference to the connection we can make to the inside of a horse.

Trust Versus Obedience

Summary: *A horse's trust comes from its understanding that yielding to a rider's idea will work out well. In contrast, obedience is the belief that not yielding to a rider's idea will be costly in terms of safety and comfort. It can be* *hard to distinguish between a horse's trust and obedience. Without trust, a horse and rider will be restricted in the quality of relationship they share.*

The notion of trust is often intertwined in the idea of partnership or a good relationship between human and horse. We expect that in all good relationships, there is a level of trust between both parties.

Even though many people talk about a horse's trust as a really important part of having a good relationship with a horse, do we really know what it means? We all know what trust means from a human perspective, but I'm not sure we know what it means from a horse's viewpoint. Do horses really understand the concept of trust in the same way we understand it?

I think trust comes from a horse's confidence that going along with our idea is going to keep them safe and comfortable. This is a process that begins with their first experience of humans and ends with their last. It is an evolving process that can go forward or backward. We can prove to a horse that we can be trusted to keep it safe and comfortable, and in the next second, prove that we can't.

People say their horse trusts them, but how do they know this? How can we differentiate between trust and obedience? I think obedience plays a big part in what we perceive to be trust. Tom Dorrance used to say that he'd like to feel like he could ride his horse up a telephone pole or down into a badger hole. Yet that willingness that Tom liked to feel in a horse, did it come from the horse having enormous trust in Tom or unquestioning obedience to him? How can one know? Are they even separable? Which comes first – obedience or trust? Is it a chicken and egg question?

Before I give you an example of what I mean, let me offer my personal definition of obedience and trust, just so we can be clear we are talking about the same thing. You may not agree with my definitions, but it will give you an idea of what I am thinking in regards to trust and obedience.

Trust is doing something because you believe that it will do you no harm.

Obedience is doing something because you believe that not doing it will be troubling.

In other words, you do something trusting it's a good idea. Or you do something out of obedience because you fear not doing it will be a bad idea.

So let's look at a real-life example of the complexity of obedience versus trust. If we have had some rain and there are puddles dotted around the ground, when my horse is wandering around the paddock it walks around each puddle to avoid stepping in them. However, when I ride my horse, it walks through each puddle that is in the path of where we are riding without hesitation or attempt to walk around them.

I do not need to guide or direct my horse to keep it straight or prevent it from avoiding the puddles. My horse walks through the puddle simply because they are in the path of where we are riding. Is this because the horse trusts me or because it is obedient and knows not to veer off course to avoid the puddles?

At first glance, I think it appears that my horse has learned its job is to go straight where I am directing it, no matter what obstacles are in the path. My horse has learned to be obedient to where I direct its thought. This would seem a natural assumption since it avoids the puddles when I am not directing it, which suggests it would not be my horse's choice to voluntarily go through a puddle. Yet, could there be a more complex explanation than that?

What if my horse walks around each puddle when I am not directing it because the confidence in itself to traverse the puddle is weak? What if it doesn't trust its own judgment to walk through water that appears to be bottomless and with unknown footing? My horse doesn't know if it will sink deeply into the puddle, or if it's slippery or rocky. What if my horse chooses to walk through the puddles when I direct it because it trusts me enough to believe I won't put it in harm's way? My horse may not have confidence in its own ability to make those judgment calls, but it may have confidence in my ability.

To put it more in human terms, imagine a small child going to school for the first time in its life. It could be very daunting for the child if mum dropped the child off at the school gate and said, "See you later". There is every chance the child would cry and put on a display because it feared the unknown that the first day of school presented.

Yet, if mum took the child into the school, introduced the teacher and sat in the class for support, the child may feel much more comfortable and less intimidated. Trust in mum, and the support she provided, could make a huge difference to how the child handled the situation.

I hear a lot about how people believe their horse trusts them, but of course, trust is not an all-or-nothing emotion. A horse may trust you enough to ride circles in an arena, but not trust you to the point of letting you ride them through a raging bushfire or across a creek.

I think the amount of trust a horse feels for a rider is one factor in limiting the degree of obedience it offers. A horse may be very obedient right up to the point where it loses trust in the rider to keep it safe. Then it's every horse and rider for himself or herself.

In my mind, there is no doubt that horses can feel trust and I believe that a good relationship is not possible without a horse and rider feeling a high degree of trust in each other. The tricky part is to know if what we think is a horse's trust is really only a horse's obedience.

You Think You Got It?

Summary: *People set their ambition to teach a horse a job. However, just because you can get the job done does not mean that you have reached a place where all is good. In* *good horsemanship, it is not enough to be able to get it done. It doesn't end there. We are limited more by our expectations, than our abilities.*

People vary in their view of the relationship they have with their horse. I guess we all have different definitions of what 'good' is and what we want from our horses. For me, I find achieving the kind of relationship I want with my horse to be very elusive. Just when I think I'm getting close, I discover it is still just out of reach. I'm looking for the degree of softness and focus that will give me the accuracy and quiet mind that I want to achieve in my work with my horse.

Like the mirage in the desert, just when you think you arrived at the water hole, you discover it's moved to a new horizon. That's why I talk about horsemanship being a journey without end.

One thing I do know is when I don't have it. Some people seem confused by this. They achieve a certain level of proficiency with their horse and think they have it worked out.

A while back I worked with a woman that told me her horse had a really good mouth and was very soft on the reins, but she rode her horse in a gag bit. When I asked her why she chose a gag, her answer was that her horse was heavy on the reins in an ordinary snaffle bit, but he was good in a gag bit. She thought she had a horse with a soft mouth, but she didn't.

I've seen people who flexed their horse's neck around every time they mounted to discourage their horse from walking away. Their horse stood still when its neck was flexed laterally. If they left the reins loose the horse walked forward as the rider mounted. They thought they had taught their horse to stand still, but they hadn't.

I saw a fellow demonstrate his horse side passing at liberty. The horse's nose was almost touching the arena fence as it side passed. If the horse had been in the middle of the arena, it would have walked forward, rather than sideways. The trainer and many of the spectators thought he had taught his horse to side pass, but he hadn't.

I know people who think they don't have a trailer-loading problem because it only takes five minutes to get their horse to walk up the ramp. Or because as long they have one person to hold the horse inside the float while another closes up the back, there is no problem. They thought their horse loaded into a trailer well, but it didn't.

It's really common to see horses that can do amazing things, but take no interest in the rider. The riders think they have a good relationship, but they don't. They think they have clarity, but they don't. They think they have softness, but they don't.

It's easy to believe that because you can get something done with a horse, you have it working well, and you have a good relationship with a horse. Just because a person is good at what they do, does not mean that what they do is good.

THE LITTLE
PRINCE

The Little Prince

Summary: *I think one of the most insightful books available to teach us about relationships is The Little Prince by Antoine de Saint-Exupery. It teaches that when we invite something into our lives, we are responsible for its care. The Little Prince also learns that the most important relationships require as much giving as it does taking.*

Since I was a kid, I've voraciously read books about training and horses in general. I have particularly been interested in studying some of the old master of dressage. However, these books never provided a window into the sort of approach to horsemanship that interests me nowadays. I've read some of the classics of horsemanship such *True Unity*, *The Thinking Horseman*, and *True Horsemanship Through Feel*. All of them are excellent books and worth reading several times.

However, I keep coming back to a book that has become one of my favourites on the subject of horses and relationships, even though it is not a horse book at all. I first read it when I was in my mid-teens, and then re-read it at least once every decade since. With each reading, I gain new insights about the relationship with horses that a human should never forget.

The book is the classic French children's book called *The Little Prince* by Antoine de Saint-Exupery. It was written in 1943, and is definitely the first book I read that offered insight into what I was missing with my relationship with horses.

It tells the story of a young boy who lives on a tiny planet not much bigger than a house. He can walk from one side to the other and see as many sunrises and sunsets as he wishes. He shares his planet with a rose that is vain and constantly demanding in a way that drives the Little Prince mad. He takes it upon himself to care for the rose. His other responsibility is to each day clean the three volcanoes that exist on his planet.

Eventually, the Little Prince leaves his home to explore the galaxy. Along the way, he meets many interesting characters among the stars with their own tales to tell and allegories to share. When he eventually gets to Earth, he meets a fox. The fox tells him, "the truth of what the eyes see can only be clearly seen by the heart," which the Little Prince understands to mean there is more to a relationship than appears on the surface.

However, the message that I most remember, that stuck with me about working with horses was when the fox told the Little Prince, ".... you are responsible forever for what you tame," and, "it is the time you have devoted to your rose that makes your rose so important".

These two messages really caused my little brain to whirl. I realized that my horse is important because I am responsible for it. The importance of a horse doesn't come from it being useful or fun or pretty or talented. The importance comes from the fact that I am responsible for it.

Even more than that, it was a huge revelation to know that I don't own a horse. I am just responsible for it. Just like a parent doesn't own a child, yet is responsible for it. The responsibility comes from inviting a horse into my life (or as the fox would say "tamed it"). It doesn't come from a bill of sale or registration papers.

The fox taught the Little Prince why the rose, despite all the trouble it caused him, was so important. And the fox taught me why each and every horse is so important.

CPSIA information can be obtained
at www.ICGtesting.com
Printed in the USA
BVHW030454100819
555530BV00001B/115/P

9 780646 930909